Marvels of China

Marvels of China

Marvels
of China

Authors: Du Feibao and Du Minglun
Translators: Kuang Peihua, Ren Lingjuan, Yu Man

CHINA TRAVEL & TOURISM PRESS

Sketch Map of China's Administrative Divisions

⊙ Urumqi

Xinjiang Uygur Autonomous Region

Gansu

Inner Mong

The Y

Yinch ⊙

Ningxia Hui
Autonomou
Region

Xining ⊙

Qinghai

Lanzhou ⊙

Gansu

Xi'a

Shaa

Tibet Autonomous Region

⊙ Lhasa

Sichuan

Chengdu ⊙

Chongqi

Chongqing ⊙

Guizhou

Guiyang ⊙

Kunming ⊙

Yunnan

Guar
Autonom

Nanr

Heilongjiang
⊙Harbin

Jilin
⊙Changchun

Shenyang
⊙
Liaoning

onomous Region

Hohhot
⊙

Beijing
Beijing★
Tianjin
⊙Tianjin
Hebei
Bohai(Sea)
Taiyuan⊙ ⊙Shijiazhuang
hanxi
Shandong
⊙Jinan

Yellow Sea

Zhengzhou⊙ Jiangsu
Henan

Anhui
ubei
Hefei⊙ ⊙Nanjing Shanghai
te River Wuhan⊙ Shanghai
Hangzhou
Zhejiang East China Sea

nan⊙
angsha Nanchang
Jiangxi
Fujian Chiwei Island
Diaoyu Island
Fuzhou
⊙Taipei

ang Guangdong
on ⊙Guangzhou Taiwan
⊙Hong Kong
Macao Hong Kong SAR

ao SAR
aikou Dongsha Islands
nan

South China Sea

Guangxi Zhuang ⊙Guangzhou Taiwan
Autonomous ⊙Region ⊙Hong Kong
Nanning Macao Hong Kong SAR
Macao SAR

⊙Haikou Dongsha
Hainan Islands

Xisha
Islands Zhongsha
Islands

Nansha
Islands

Zengmu
Reef

South China Sea Islands

Authors: Du Feibao and Du Minglun
Translators: Kuang Peihua, Ren Lingjuan and Yu Man
Managing Editor: Tan Yan (lyty2006@163.com)
Printing Supervisor: Feng Dongqing
Art Designer: Wu Tao
Photographers: Bian Zhiwu, Tan Ming, Zhang Zhaoji, Yang Yin, Lu Yan, Chen Keyin, Wang Jingui, Zhou Xinjun, Yang Yang, Wang Wenbo, Jiang Jingyu, Wang Yan, Dong Li and Du Feibao
(Some of the photos in the book are provided by Colphoto, the Panorama Media (Beijing) Ltd. and Chinanews. We would like to express our heartfelt gratitude to them.)

Published by China Travel & Tourism Press
(A9 Jianguomennei Dajie, Beijing 100005,China)
Printed in the People's Republic of China

Foreword

We planned to write a book about the marvels of China a long time ago. The idea originated with a French friend of mine, who mailed me a book (*Les Merveilles du Monde*) with both pictures and text. That beautiful book helped us have a good understanding of the most renowned scenic spots and historical sites in the world without even leaving the country. However, the tourist attractions of China included in the French book are few in number — the Great Wall, former Imperial Palace and Temple of Heaven, etc. — thus inspiring us to write our own book — *Marvels of China*.

How many marvels does China actually have? It seems there are no precise statistics. All the marvels included in this book are divided into two parts: "Natural Marvels of China" and "Architectural Marvels of China," which are the most important parts of China's tourism resources. At the beginning, when we discussed the book with the publisher, we planned to write about 150 marvels of China, including about 50 natural marvels, and 100 architectural marvels. Certainly, China embraces more than 150 marvels, but as some scenic marvels are in remote areas difficult of access, we had to omit them, however painful it was.

How to decide on each marvel was the key to this book. Based on many selections and constant reference to the comments of experts, we adopted the following steps:

First, classifying scenic spots and historical sites into different categories. The natural marvels of China are divided into high mountains, deserts, lakes, forests of peaks, Danxia landforms, canyons, waterfalls, Yardan landforms, caves, glaciers, forests, grasslands, marshlands and wetlands, coasts, islands, tides, etc. The architectural marvels of China are divided into the Great Wall, cities, palaces, temples, gardens, mausoleums, guild halls, academies, ordinary people's residences, water-conservancy projects, bridges, prisons, tunnels, pagodas, grottoes, Taoist architecture, Islamic architecture, museums, etc.

Second, deciding on the standards for the marvels of China. After referring to many domestic and foreign books on scenic and historical marvels, we decided to take "oddness, uniqueness and beauty" as the standards for selecting the marvels of China. On the basis of this classification, we selected the most unusual, special and beautiful from a large number of scenic spots and historical sites in China. If a type of scenic spot is rich in contents, we would select more marvels from that category, and if some types of scenic spots are poor in contents, we would select fewer marvels from them. The types not up to standard would be ignored.

Third, comparing Chinese marvels with those of foreign countries. We discovered that when selecting the natural marvels of China, we could compare them with those of other countries; but when selecting the architectural marvels of China, we could hardly compare them with foreign ones, because every country has its own architectural style and cultural connotations. In spite of this, we maintained that it was necessary for them to make such a comparison, so as to avoid subjectivism and unilateralism. In addition, when selecting the architectural marvels of China, we paid more attention to ancient Chinese architectural structures than to new ones. This is somewhat regrettable. Hopefully, we shall remedy this in the future.

China is one of the countries with the richest tourism resources in the world. *Marvels of China* introduces the most famous scenic spots and historical sites in this vast and ancient land. Hence, it is an important reference book and gives readers a good understanding of the best tourist destinations in China.

Over the past few decades, we have traveled all over the country, and have written several books on tourism for China Travel & Tourism Press. For this book, we made painstaking efforts to collect materials, select marvels, choose pictures and write the text. This book, with both pictures and text, is very informative and useful for foreign readers. Any comments and suggestions on the book *Marvels of China* are warmly welcome.

We would like to express our heartfelt gratitude for the great support we received from China Travel & Tourism Press in the publishing of this book, to all the photographers who provided beautiful pictures, and to the translators from the China International Publishing Group. It is because of their diligent work that we can introduce China's excellent tourism culture to the world, and let people of other countries appreciate the fascinating Chinese sights.

Authors
April 9, 2007, Beijing

Contents

Foreword

✳   ✳   ✳   ✳   ✳   ✳   ✳   ✳

Part Two   Architectural Marvels of China

Chinese Cities

Chinese Temples

Chinese Gardens

Chinese Mausoleums

Chinese Buddhist Temples

Chinese Buddhist Pagodas

Part One Natural Marvels of China

第一部分　中国自然景观

China is situated in the eastern part of the Asian continent on the western coast of the Pacific Ocean. China's land area covers 9.6 million square kilometers, and its sea area, 4.73 million square kilometers. China is the largest country in Asia, and the third largest country in the world. Looking down over the land of China from the sky, you will see China's topography like a huge ladder, rising step by step from east to west. The vast territory, varied landforms, numerous rivers and lakes, long and undulating coasts, fertile seas, lush and green forests and delicate scenery have given birth to a number of natural scenic wonders on the vast land of China.

It is very difficult to give a statistical figure on how many natural wonders China actually has. When selecting China's natural wonders for this book, the author paid attention to the comparison between the landforms of China with those of foreign countries. Hence this book contains the natural wonders unique to China, as well as those whose scale is larger than that of foreign countries. Selecting the natural wonders of China through this method will probably help reduce one-sidedness and blindness.

High Moun-
tains in China
中国高山概述

China is home to many mountains. According to statistics, the famous high mountains in China number over 200 in total. The principal mountains in China generally fall into the following three types:

First, traditional famous mountains
第一，传统名山

In ancient China, the emperors claimed to be the "sons of Heaven." "To repay Heaven for kindness," they often took the magnificent and precipitous mountains as the auspicious signs, where they set up altars to offer sacrifices to Heaven. The first feudal emperor in Chinese history holding a large-scale ceremony to confer a feudal title upon a mountain is Emperor Qin Shihuang, First Emperor of the Qin Dynasty. To ensure that the country was prosperous and the people lived in peace, the emperors of the successive dynasties frequently held activities to confer feudal titles on mountains. Finally the five most famous mountains of China emerged, i.e., Mount Tai in the east; Mount Huashan in the west; Mount Hengshan in the north; Mount Songshan in the central; and Mount Hengshan in the south. Since then the "five sacred mountains" have enjoyed a high reputation throughout the world, and become the pronouns of renowned mountains in China.

Second, the famous Buddhist mountains
第二，佛教名山

An old Chinese saying goes: "The monks occupy most of the famous mountains." When the emperors of past ages were busy conferring titles upon famous mountains, monks speeded up building temples in the mountains across the country for practicing Buddhism. Consequently, the "four famous Buddhist mountains" in China came into forth, i.e., Mount Emei in Sichuan, Mount Wutai in Shanxi, Mount Putuo in Zhejiang and Mount Jiuhua in Anhui. As Taoists are particular about tranquility and prefer to being away from the turmoil of the world, a great number of famous Taoist mountains, represented by Mount Wudang, emerged as the times demanded. It proves that the famous religious mountains in China are actually the models of the perfect combination of China's natural and cultural legacies.

Third, newly discovered mountains
第三，新发现的大山

Along with the progress of society, the development of science and technology, and the emergence of mountaineering and tourism, China has found a number of new mountains in modern times. Some of them are suitable for climbing, and the others, for sightseeing. In history, the Chinese people did not give sufficient attention to the places where groups of mountains gather, because of their high elevations and poor transport facilities. In modern times, when explorers, mountaineers, travelers, geologists and meteorologists traveled to or made inspections of western China, they constantly discovered clusters of high mountains and glaciers, as well as a great number of world-level natural wonders. Though they are not famed, they are more magnificent and beautiful than the famous mountains.

Mount Tai – the Ancestor of Chinese Mountains

泰山——被封为中国的"岱宗"

Situated in Tai'an City in east China, about 103 kilometers south of Jinan City, Shandong Province, Mount Tai ranks first of China's five sacred mountains as mentioned above. As Mount Tai is located in east China, it is also called the Eastern Great Mountain, with a total area of 426 square kilometers, and its main peak is 1,532 meters above sea level. In ancient times, people regarded the east as the place where the new replaced the old and all things on earth grew in spring. Hence Mount Tai enjoys a reputation of being the "leader and the most respectful of the five great mountains." In ancient times, the first thing for an emperor to do on ascending to the throne was to climb Mount Tai to confer a title on Mount Tai and pray to heaven and earth for times of peace and prosperity.

Mount Tai was formed in the Archean Era, about 2.45 billion to 2.5 billion years ago. Accordingly, Mount Tai is also called "Daizong," meaning the ancestor of all the high mountains in China.

Since ancient times, Mount Tai has been known as a sacred mountain. Legend has it that, Mount Tai was the place where the head of Pan Gu, creator of the universe in Chinese mythology, was located. Pan Gu, born before the separation of heaven from earth, is the earliest ancestor of human beings. After his death, all parts of his body were turned into mountains, the sun, the moon, rivers, seas, grasses, trees and other things; and his head was turned into Mount Tai. An ancient saying goes: "Heaven and earth merge at Mount Tai." It was said that 72 Chinese emperors of different dynasties made pilgrimages to this mountain, and every pilgrimage would leave behind some temples, statues, inscriptions and stone carvings. Now over 20 clusters of ancient architectural structures, and more than 2,000 historical and cultural sites can be found in the mountain. When climbing Mount Tai, Confucius once said: "At the top of Eastern Mountain, the state of Lu seems small; and at the summit of Mount Tai, the whole country looks small." Du Fu, a celebrated poet of the Tang Dynasty (618-907), once wrote a poem

titled "Gazing at Mount Tai," reading: "I must
ascend the mountain's crest;/It dwarfs all
peaks under my feet."

Now Mount Tai is a famed tourist attrac-
tion in China. There are two ascents of the
mountain: the East Route and the West Route.
The two routes meet at the Gate Half-way to
Heaven, and then lead directly to the summit.
The main tourist attractions in Mount Tai in-
clude the Gate Half-way to Heaven, Yunbu
Bridge, Sun Watching Peak, Moon Watching
Peak, and so on. The four wonders of Mount
Tai are the Sunrise from the East, the Sunset
Glow, the Sea of Clouds and the Golden Belt
Along the Yellow River. Mount Tai preserves
a great number of cultural relics and historical
sites of the past dynasties, which are rare
in the world. Mount Tai has been included in
the World Heritage List by the UNESCO.

Mount Emei – a Great Mountain Rising from a Basin

峨眉山——从盆地里升起的大山

Located in the Sichuan Basin in southwest China, about 200 kilometers south of Chengdu, Mount Emei undulates 23 kilometers from south to north, with an area of 115 square kilometers. The Ten-Thousand-Buddha Summit, the highest peak of Mount Emei, rises 3,099 meters above sea level, 2,600 meters higher than the plain at the eastern foot of the mountain. Several hundred million years ago, Mount Emei sank and rose twice, and it was not until 70 million years ago, the Emei fault zone was formed during the course of rise, giving birth to a number of natural wonders, such as peaks rising one higher than another, and deep and secluded valleys.

Mount Emei is one of the four sacred Buddhist mountains in China. Since ancient times, its charming scenery has won it the name of

"Emei, the greatest beauty under Heaven." Now there are over 70 temples in the mountain. Climbers of the mountain start at the Devotion to the Country Temple at the foot of the mountain and reach the Golden Summit, totaling over 60 kilometers. Scenes along the way consist of the temples and natural scenic spots, which are tucked away in the green woods, presenting a beautiful painting scroll featuring "freshness, tranquility, beauty and elegance." The Ten-Thousand-Year Temple is one of the major temples in Mount Emei. A doomed building with small stupas on it, the temple is 16 meters wide and 16 meters high, built of bricks without beams and wood.

Within the Hall towers a huge bronze statue of Samantabhadra (Bodhisattva of Universal Benevolence) mounted on a white elephant with six tusks. Cast in the fifth year of the Xingguo reign period (980) of the Northern Song Dynasty, the statue is 7.3 meters high and weighs 62 tons — an excellent example of the fine technique of ancient Chinese artisans. Standing at the Golden Summit, tourists can appreciate the four scenic wonders of Mount Emei — the sunrise, Buddha's halo, the sea of clouds, and the Holy Lamp. Mount Emei has been included in the World Heritage List by the UNESCO.

Mount Huangshan – the Most Beautiful Mountain in the Eyes of the Chinese People

黄山——中国人心目中最美的山

Huangshan one of the most famous scenic spots in China, as well as the world-renowned tourist attraction.

Mount Huangshan boasts 72 towering peaks, of which Heavenly Capital (Tiandu) Peak, Lotus Peak and Bright Summit are the three main peaks, with an elevation of over 1,841 meters. Spectacular rocks, odd-shaped pines, a sea of clouds and hot springs are known as the "four wonders" of Mount Huangshan. Xu Xiake, a famous geologist of the Ming Dynasty (1368-1644), once spoke highly of Mount Huangshan: "You won't wish to visit any other mountains after seeing the five most important mountains in China; and you won't wish to visit any other four most important mountains in China after returning from Mount Huangshan." The saying has become a popular praise of Mount Huangshan among the Chinese people. Mount Huangshan enjoys a high popularity in China as well as in the world. Mount Huangshan has been included in the World Heritage List by the UNESCO.

Mount Huangshan is located in Huangshan City, Anhui Province in central China. Legend has it that the Emperor Huangdi (or Yellow Emperor), the first ancestor of the Chinese nation, once cultivated his mind and prepared herbal medicine in the mountain, hence the name. Mount Huangshan has a circumference of 250 kilometers, of which 154 kilometers are picturesque, making Mount

Mount Qomolangma
– the "Third Pole on Earth"

珠穆朗玛峰——被称为"地球第三极"

Located in Tingri County, Tibet on the border between China and Nepal, Mount
Qomolangma is the main peak of the
Himalayas, with an elevation of 8,844.43
meters. Hence it is the highest peak in the
world. Scientists call Mount Qomolangma the
"Third Pole on Earth." In the Tibetan

language, Qomolangma means Mother Goddess of the Universe. Shaped like a pyramid,
the mountaintop is covered with snow all the
year round. Mount Qomolangma has given
birth to numerous huge glaciers, cirques and
horns. The longest glacier lasts 26 kilometers,
presenting picturesque scenery. If it is fine

visitors can view a cloud ball in milky white moving slowly to the east, like a white flag fluttering in the blue skies. It is the flag cloud, a famed scenic wonder of Mount Qomolangma. To mountaineers, the flag cloud is a very important sign, which shows the wind-force at the mountaintop. If the flag cloud is even with the mountaintop, it indicates about force 9 wind. The exploration of and research on Mount Qomolangma have always attracted adventurers and scientists from all the countries in the world. At the foot of Mount Qomolangma lies the Rongpo Monastery, 5,154 meters above sea level, which is the temple with the highest eleva-tion in the world. At the Rongpo Monastery, visitors can have a nice view of the scenic wonders in Mount Qomolangma. The Chinese Academy of Sciences has organized large-scale scientific investigation groups time and again to make inspections of the mountain, and important scientific data have been obtained. In 2005 Mount Qomolangma was named one of the most beautiful places in China. Now it is a famous tourist attraction in China for mountaineering and sightseeing. The period from April to June every year is the best season to visit Mount Qomolangma.

Kangrinboqe Peak – the Sacred Mountain of the Tibetan People

冈仁波齐峰——西藏人民心目中的神山

Located in Burang County, Ngari Prefecture of Tibet in southwest China, Kangrinboqe Peak is the main peak of the Gangdise Mountains, also known as Holy Mountain or Sacred Mountain. With an elevation of 6,638 meters, Kangrinboqe Peak is one of the famous sacred Buddhist places in Tibet.

In the shape of an olive, Kangrinboqe Peak penetrates into the clouds, with the top capped with snow all the year round. At dusk, when the sunset glow shines on the plateau, the crimsoned snow-covered peak looks like

burning in the universe. According to the records in the Sanskrit documents, as early as in 2000 B.C., the Gangdise Mountains was designated as Sacred Mountain. In the 11th century when Atisha, a Buddhist master of Bengal, and his entourage came to pay homage to the Sacred Mountain, colorful clouds suddenly gathered to surround the peak, and the true body of Buddha appeared on the clouds time and again. After that, many Buddhist believers come here to pay homage to the mountain and practice Buddhism every year. Now a great number of caves where Buddhist believers went into Buddhist self-discipline can be found in the mountain. A saying popular among Buddhist believers goes: Walking round the sacred mountain once will help one get rid of all sins in one's life; walking round the sacred mountain 10 times will help one avoid going to the hell; and walking round the sacred mountain 100 times will help one become Buddha and go to Heaven. On the way to Kangrinboqe Peak, a continuous flow of Buddhists to pay homage to the sacred mountain can be seen every year, becoming a unique scenic sight.

Buddhism takes Mount Sumeru as the world's center, but most people believe that it is just a fabricated mountain. Probably Kangrinboqe Peak is the true sacred mountain. A lot of mountains in Tibet are regarded as sacred mountains, but only Kangrinboqe Peak is taken as the King of Sacred Mountains by all the sects of Tibetan Buddhism.

Chinese Glaciers

中国冰川概述

Generally, the glaciers in China fall into three categories: Marine glaciers, sub-continental glaciers and continental glaciers. According to the shapes of the glaciers, they can also be divided into valley glaciers, suspended glaciers, cirque glaciers and tabular glaciers.

According to the investigations and statistics by experts, China now has over 46,000 glaciers, which are mainly distributed in sparsely populated western China. Glaciers are spirits hidden deeply in the mountains, and are scenic wonders that human beings have the most difficult in approaching them in nature.

Rongpu Glacier – a Scenic Wonder on the Roof of the World

绒布冰川——世界屋脊的奇观

Situated in Rongpu Valley north of Mount Qomolangma in Tingri County, about 240 kilometers southwest of Xigaze in Tibet, Rongpu Glacier lies in a vast region ranging from 5,300 to 6,300 meters at the foot of Mount Qomolangma. The glacier extends about 22 kilometers, and covers an area of about 85 square kilometers. The glacier tongue is about 1.4 kilometers wide on average and 120 meters thick, the thickest reaching over 300 meters. As one of the most vigorous and majestic scenic spots, the glacier region presents various kinds of wonderful sights, such as the forest of ice pagodas, glacial lakes, ice precipices, ice caves and ice crevices. Standing in the glacier, people will feel as if they came to a fairyland with richly decorated jade palaces. According to the assessments by glacier experts, Rongpu Glacier is the best-developed and best-preserved glacier in the world, of which the forest of ice pagodas is a world-level scenic wonder.

Mount Tumuer Glaciers Add Beauty to the Tianshan Mountains

托木尔峰冰川——天山因它而美丽

Located in Wensu County north of Aksu City in the Xinjiang Uygur Autonomous Region, Mount Tumuer is the highest peak of the Tianshan Mountains, 7,443 meters above sea level. With an area of over 2,800 square kilometers, Mount Tumuer has a total of over 500 glaciers, being one of the largest glaciers in China. Mount Tumuer is surrounded by layer upon layer of snow-covered ranges, which look like flying jade dragons glittering cold light under sunshine in a distance, full of power and grandeur. Walking on the glaciers, visitors can view ice mushrooms, lakes and caves. Sometimes, visitors can hear underground rivers gurgling on, or a huge and horrible sound of the collapse of glaciers if the temperature goes up. The Chinese mountaineering party climbed to the top of Mount Tumuer twice in July 25 and 30, 1977, respectively. Now the mysterious and gorgeous scenes of the Mount Tumuer Glacier attract the eyes of numerous mountaineers, travelers, adventurers and photographers in the world. Every year, July and August are the best travel seasons.

Conch Gully Glacier
– Spring in Winter

海螺沟冰川——冬天里的春天

Located in Moxi Township, 52 kilometers south of Luding County on the eastern slope of Konggar Mountain of Sichuan Province in southwest China, the Conch Gully is the only glacier forest park in China, 30.7 kilometers long, which covers an area of 16 square kilometers. The Conch Gully is well known in the world because that "the gully presents exquisite beauties of four seasons in a day, and weather differs distinctively within a short distance of ten miles."

Konggar Mountain contains over 100 glaciers, of which Conch Gully Glacier is the largest and most magnificent. With an elevation of 2,850 meters, Conch Gully Glacier is 14.7 kilometers long, and two kilometers wide, and stretches into the primitive forests for six kilometers. The coexistence of a glacier and a forest is a weird and rare phenomenon in the world. The most magnificent sight on the glacier is a large ice waterfall, over 1,000 meters high and over 1,000 meters wide, which looks like a huge silvery screen hung in the sky. At the end of the glacier is the glacier tongue, which has moved down with lumps of ice and has gradually been melted, forming various types of wonderful ice scenic spots, such as ice caves, lakes, bridges, doors, ladders, tables and so on. All of them are sparkling, crystal-clear and appealing. In addition, Conch Gully gathers four kinds of springs with boiling, hot, warm and cold waters, the temperature ranging from 50℃ to 80℃. Some hot spring bathing places and alpine hot spring swimming pools can be found in the gully. Every year, the periods from March to May, and from October to December are the best travel seasons.

Chinese Hoodoos

中国峰林概述

The hoodoos refer to tall and erect landforms, mainly represented by forests of stones, sands and earth. The hoodoos in China are mainly distributed in the Yunnan-Guizhou Plateau in the southwest of the country, especially in the regions with the karst landforms. After the land had been exposed to the weather, and the surface water had kept permeated into the ground for thousands of years, porous limestone were gradually melted by water to form fairly solid rocks, sandstones and sandy soils on the land, looking like forests, which are very fascinating scenic wonders in nature.

Stone Forest with Count-less Stone Pillars

石林——还没数清的石柱

Located in Shilin County, about 90 kilometers east of Kunming City, Yunnan Province in southwest China, Stone Forest was formed in the Palaeozoic era, with a typically developed karst landforms. Stone Forest covers an area of over 26,000 hectares and extends about five kilometers, including a number of scenic spots, such as Larger Stone Forest, Lesser Stone Forest, Outer Stone Forest, Stone Forest Lake, Underground Stone Forest in Purple Cloud Cave, Lion Hill, Lion Pond, Sword Peak Pond, Lotus Pond, Zang Lake and Dadieshui Waterfall.

Stone Forest is composed of oddly shaped stones formed by a layer of eroded limestone, known as the "karst landforms." Some 200 million years ago, this area was submerged under a thick layer of limestone at the bottom of the sea. Later, the movement of the earth's crust caused the sea bottom to thrust upward

Chinese Hoodoos

and became land. Owing to solvent action, long deep cracks developed in the limestone, and rainwater running through the cracks gradually eroded the stone into the present shapes, such as stone peaks, stone pillars, stalactites, stalagmites, eroded depressions, underground rivers and underground caves. Some stone peaks and pillars are 30-40 meters high. A number of huge black stone peaks and pillars rise straight from the ground and soar into the sky, looking just like a dense forest in a distance, fascinating and magnificent.

Scenic Lijiang River
– a Gallery of Natural Landscapes

桂林漓江风光——山水相依的画廊

Located in Guilin in the Guangxi Zhuang Autonomous Region in southwest China, the Lijiang River starts from Xing'an in the north and ends at Yangshuo in the south, over 100 kilometers long in total. Due to the development of the limestone landforms, the erosion of underground water and the movement of the earth's crust, a great number of hills in Guilin rose from the ground, showing various kinds of shapes. Some look like jade bamboo shoots; some, like green screens; and the

Chinese Hoodoos

others, like humps and elephants. Guilin also boasts a number of karst caverns, where lots of scenic attractions are formed by stalactites, stalagmites, stone curtains, stone pillars and stone flowers. Since ancient times, the city of Guilin has enjoyed the reputation of having the country's most beautiful scenery. Its main scenic spots include Folded Brocade Hill, Elephant Trunk Hill, Wave Tamping Hill, Solitary Beauty Peak, Reed Flute Cave, Seven Star Rock, etc. The Lijiang River, the main river in Guilin, is like a jade belt surrounding the city. A visit to Guilin would not be complete without a boat excursion down the Lijiang River to Yangshuo, totaling 83 kilometers. This is like sailing down a scroll on which is painted a traditional Chinese landscape of green bamboo, dense forests, cottages scattered here and there, fertile fields, oddly shaped peaks and limpid running waters. Han Yu, a famous poet of the Tang Dynasty (618-907), once wrote a poem to sing highly of scenic Guilin: "The river is like a green belt; and the hills resemble jade hairpins."

✳ ✳ ✳ ✳ ✳ ✳ ✳ ✳

Wulingyuan Scenic and Historic Interest Area with 3,103 Peaks

武陵源风光——谁能数清 3103 座峰

Located in the northern suburbs of Zhangjiajie, over 40 kilometers from Zhangjiajie City, Hunan Province, the Wulingyuan Scenic and Historic Interest Area has a total area of 264 square kilometers, and consists of three major scenic zones — Suoxi Valley, Tianzi Mountain and Zhangjiajie National Forest Park.

Over 380 million years' geological changes in Wulingyuan gave birth to unique quartz sandstone peaks and valleys, something rarely seen anywhere else on earth. The Wulingyuan Scenic and Historic Interest Area integrates peaks,

waters, forests and caves, takes 3,103 peaks in various odd and complex shapes as the mainstay, and features weird peaks, secluded valleys, deep forests and mysterious caves, presenting a fascinating natural landscape painting and enjoying a reputation of being "No. 1 Marvelous Mountain on Earth," and the "Memento of Earth." The three major scenic zones in Wulingyuan are an integral whole, but each has its own characteristics. Zhangjiajie Park is known for its oddly shaped rocks, tranquil waters and elegant forests; Suoxi Valley Scenic Zone boasts green peaks rising one higher than another, running streams, limpid lakes and secluded caves; and Tianzi Mountain occupies a commanding position, with a forest of peaks, deep and serene valleys, a wide field of vision and clear gradation. The Wulingyuan Scenic and Historic Interest Area has been included in the List of World Heritages by the UNESCO.

Chinese Canyons

中国峡谷概述

A country with numerous mountains and canyons, China ranks first in the world in the number of canyons. The canyons introduced in this book are the deepest, longest, widest and weirdest ones in China. The canyons are divided into dry and water canyons. A canyon with a river presents a magnificent sight, because rivers are the blood of the land, and the soul of canyons. A canyon with waterfalls shows fascinating and picturesque scenery.

Canyons

Yarlungzangbo Grand Canyon – the Largest Canyon in the World

雅鲁藏布大峡谷——世界第一大峡谷

Lying at the foot of Namjagbarwa Peak in Mainling County of Tibet, the Yarlungzangbo Canyon was discovered by the Chinese scientists in 1994, and was formally named the Yarlungzangbo Grand Canyon by China in 1998. It is well known because it was the last canyon discovered in the world.

The Yarlungzangbo River runs from west to east between the Himalayas and the Gangdise Mountains; cuts through the Himalayas at the inlet in Pai Township of Mainling County, with an average volume of flow of 2,000 cubic meters/second; enters Medog County after forming a unique U-shaped bend around Namjagbarwa Peak; and flows out from the outlet at Baxika, with an average volume of flow of 5,200 cubic meters/second, thus forming the Yarlungzangbo Grand Canyon. The canyon is 504.6 kilometers long; and the deepest spot is located at Zangrong Village where Namjagbarwa Peak meets the Yarlungzangbo River, 6,009 meters

deep. The deepest spot on one side is close to Dego Village, 7,057 meters deep. The average depth of the canyon is 2,268 meters; and the average depth of the core section is 2,673 meters. The average volume of flow of the river water in the canyon is 4,425 cubic meters/second, and the flow speed reaches 16 meters/second. According to the judgment by experts, the Yarlungzangbo Grand Canyon is the champion in the world in terms of length, width, depth, flow, magnificence, steepness, weirdness, elegance and mystery, and is the last mysterious site on earth. One who has not gone into it cannot say that one has viewed the most magnificent canyon in the world.

* * * * * * * *

Tiger Jumping Gorge on the Jinsha River – Can a Tiger Really Jump over the Gorge?

金沙江虎跳峡──老虎真的能跳过峡谷吗?

The Tiger Jumping Gorge is located in the northeast of Stone Drum Town, 68 kilometers west of Lijiang Naxi Autonomous County in Yunnan Province. The Jinsha River is on the upper reaches of the Yangtze River, with deep and swift currents. The river runs down from Tacheng to the northwest of Lijiang, and turns to the north at Stone Drum Town to cut through the snow-covered Yulong and Haba mountains and form a magnificent gorge. Here the tributary of the Jinsha River is only 30 to 60 meters wide. Legend has it that a huge tiger once jumped over the gorge, hence the name. The gorge is about 16 kilometers long; the river is flanked by straight and tall cliffs; and the mountain ranges are over 3,000 meters above the river. All these make it one of the deepest gorges in the world. The mighty waters of the Jinsha River roar down, and rush through seven steep ridges; and the drop in elevation between the upper and down gorge outlets is 170 meters. The water surface on

the upper reaches is as level as a mirror, but the waters at the "Tiger Jumping Stone" are surging, like a huge river falling down from heaven, accompanied by a thundering sound, a magnificent scene that astonishes every viewer.

The Tiger Jumping Gorge is an important component part of the Lijiang Yulong Snow-covered Mountain Scenic Zone, which attracts many people to make investigations and do sightseeing every year.

Kuqa Grand Canyon
– the "Red Grand Canyon"

库车大峡谷——被称为 "红色大峡谷"

About 64 kilometers north of the seat of Kuqa County at the southern foot of the Tianshan Mountains in Xinjiang in northwest China, the Kuqa Grand Canyon is called the "Keziliya Canyon" by the local people, meaning the "Red Cliffs." The canyon, about five kilometers long, consists of a main canyon and seven branches. In general, the canyon is 150 to 200 meters deep; the highest peak is 2,049 meters tall; and the narrowest spot only allows two people to pass by. Under the bright sunshine, red sandstones glisten in the secluded canyon full of oddly shaped rocks, presenting a unique and enchanting scene. According to the experts' opinions, the Kuqa Grand Canyon is a unique one in China, which consists of red and brownish rocks, showing manly beauty as compared with other canyons with a gloomy atmosphere. Lots of people call it "Red Grand Canyon." In the canyon, tourists can find a great number of natural sculptures, which were carved by melted water of snow and ice from the Tianshan Mountains. Some look like immortals; some resemble beasts; and the others are like old men holding sticks. A natural stone crack is named "One Thread Sky." At dawn or duck when winds rise and clouds scud, the canyon changes colors rapidly, making viewers feel mysterious.

Jiuzhaigou
– the "Fairyland on Earth"

九寨沟——被称为"童话世界"

Situated in Longkang Township, Jiuzhaigou County, Sichuan Province, Jiuzhaigou (Nine Village Valley) is home to nine Tibetan villages, hence the name. With a total area of 720 square kilometers, Jiuzhaigou consists of three main valleys — Shuzheng, Rize and Zechawa, which are surrounded by over 10 peaks covered with snow all the year round. The "Y"-shaped valley embraces 114 terraced lakes of different sizes. Between the lakes are 17 waterfalls, 47 springs, five travertine shoals and over 10 snow-capped peaks. It is a natural landscape rare in the world. The wooden Tibetan houses, waterwheels, prayer flags, and ancient and unsophisticated Tibetan customs in Jiuzhaigou form unique places of historic and cultural interest. Jiuzhaigou enjoys a reputation of being the "Wonderland" and the "Land of Peach Blossoms." Jiuzhaigou has

been included in the World Heritage List by the UNESCO.

Nuorilang Waterfall in the Jiuzhaigou Valley Scenic and Historic Interest Area is one of the large travertine waterfalls in China,

which is hung at the fault of Jiuzhaigou Valley. The waterfall is over 300 meters wide at maximum. As the waterfall is located in a forest, waters fall down from a calm lake, go slowly through the forests and shoals, dash against protruding rocks midway and explode into millions of silvery tiny beads, presenting a piece of wide colorful brocade woven by nature.

* * * * * * * *

Huanglong with Multicolored Lakes

黄龙——地球上真的有彩池吗

Situated in Huanglong Township, about 60 kilometers east of Songpan County in Sichuan Province in southwest China, Huanglong Valley has three small temples, so it is also called

Chinese Canyons

"Huanglong Temple." Huanglong lies at the foot of Xuebaoding Mountain, the main peak of the Minshan Mountains, with an elevation of 5,588 meters. The valley is about 3.6 kilometers long, 30-170 meters wide, and 3,160-3,574 meters above sea level. The earth's surface is covered with a thick layer of travertine. Under the sunshine, the valley looks like a huge golden dragon crouching among a vast sea of forests, hence the name Huanglong "Yellow Dragon." In the valley, visitors can find various kinds of travertine scenic spots, such as travertine ponds, shoals, waterfalls, caves and dykes, of which the most attractive are the colorful travertine ponds in different sizes and exotic shapes, known as five-colored ponds. It also boasts eight beautifully shaped groups of ponds, with over 3,400 colorful ponds sparking in the sunshine. Some look like bright mirrors; some are like jade plates; and the others are like jadeites and colorful butterflies. Every visitor will gasp in admiration at the fascinating scenery. The Huanglong Scenic and Historic Interest Area, a natural scenic wonder rarely seen in the world, has been included in the World Heritage List by the UNESCO.

Chinese
Waterfalls

中国瀑布概述

A waterfall consists three key elements: volume of flow, drop in elevation and width, of which the volume of flow is the most important, especially the annual volume of flow. China has a large number of waterfalls, but only a few of them are known as scenic wonders. Some waterfalls that rely on the reservoirs on the upper reaches to regulate the volume of flow should be regarded as artificial or semi-artificial waterfalls. Only natural beauty is true beauty.

The Tsangpo Badong Waterfalls in Tibet, and the Hukou Waterfall on the Yellow River, the most famous waterfalls in China, can only occupy small places among the famous waterfalls in the world.

Waterfalls

Tsangpo Badong Water-falls – the Most Difficult for People to Approach

藏布巴东瀑布群——人类最难接近的大瀑布

The Tsangpo Badong Waterfalls is near Namjagbarwa Peak in Mainling County in the core no-man's land of the Yarlungzangbo Grand Canyon. The 20-km-long gorge from Xingla Mountain in the west to the outlet of the Palungzangbo River, a branch of the Yarlungzangbo River, is home to four large groups of waterfalls, a unique scene in China, and a rare scene in the world. Of them the Tsangpo Badong Waterfalls is the most magnificent. The Tsangpo Badong Waterfalls is composed of three cascades, of which the one on the upper reaches is called Tsangpo Badong. In the low-water season, the Tsangpo Badong Waterfalls is 117.7 meters wide, with a drop of 33 meters. Water falls down from a steep rock in the center of the river into a deep pond with a flow rate of 1,900 cubic meters/

second, presenting a scene of waves breaking and foaming, and white chick mist rising from the river. At this moment, the whole river looks like a white silk, making people feel as if the rocks on both banks would collapse at any time. When continuing to flow forward, water is blocked by a steep cliff. Hence, running water is forced to turn to the left, rush down from narrower cracks on both side of the steep cliff and disappear from the back of the cliff. It is the Tsangpo Bandong Waterfalls. In the high-water season, the waterfalls look more magnificent. However because of the precipitous location, no one has even gone close to it, and it is even harder for scientists to make an on-the-site survey. According to the opinions of experts, the Tsangpo Badong Waterfalls, full of power and grandeur, is the most magnificent, most primitive and most mysterious waterfall in China, and ranks first among all the waterfalls in the country.

* * * * * * * *

Hukou Waterfall on the Yellow River – the Only Yellow Waterfall on Earth

黄河壶口瀑布——世界独一无二的黄色瀑布

The Hukou Waterfall on the Yellow River is between Jixian County of Shanxi Province and Yichuan County of Shaanxi Province in central China. Hukou is the most perilous section of the Yellow River Gorge, over 60 kilometers long. On the rocks at the riverbed, there is a huge trough, 30 meters wide and about 50 meters deep. Waters from the Yellow River fall down directly into the trough, just like water being poured out from a flask mouth, giving birth to rolling and roaring waves and a deafening sound that can be heard several miles away.

Legend has it that if a pig falls down from Hukou, all the hairs on the pig will be thoroughly cleaned after it emerges on the lower reaches. It proves that the momentum of the Hukou Waterfall is astonishing. In ancient China, when boats reached Hukou, boatmen had to embark off their ships and pulled them on the bank so as to detour around the waterfall, hence the saying "boats on the land." The Hukou Waterfall is a unique waterfall in the world running with silt, the most famous natural wonder on the Yellow River, and a generous gift given to China by nature.

Huangguoshu Waterfall
— the Most Famous Waterfall in China

黄果树瀑布——中国最著名的瀑布

The Huangguoshu Waterfall is situated on the Baishui River, 15 kilometers southwest of the seat of Zhenning County, and about 160 kilometers west of Guiyang City, Guizhou Province. Surrounded by range upon range of mountains, the Baishui River flows down from the midway of the mountains, with great momentum and surging waves. The bed of the Baishui River is like a staircase descending step by step, forming nine falls at each step, of which the Huangguoshu Waterfall is the largest, about

81 meters wide. The waterfall rushes down from the top of precipices, and pours into the Rhinoceros Pool. As the roaring river drops from a height of 68 meters, it sends up myriads of sprays over 20 meters high, accompanied by deafening sound. Behind the waterfall is a water curtain cave, which has six widows, five halls and three springs. Walking in the cave, tourists can appreciate the hanging waterfall from the windows, a scenic marvel indeed. Now Huangguoshu is a famous tourist attraction in China. As it was developed quite earlier, it enjoys a reputation of being the most famous waterfall in China. In 2005, the Huangguoshu Waterfall was named one of the most beautiful places in China.

※　　　※　　　※　　　※　　　※　　　※　　　※　　　※

Detian Waterfall – a Scenic Wonder on the Border Between China and Viet Nam

德天瀑布——中越边境线上的奇观

Located in Detian Village, Daxin County, about 200 kilometers west of Nanning City of the Guangxi Zhuang Autonomous Region in southwest China, the Detian Waterfall is the second largest transnational waterfall. The waterfall is over 200 meters wide at maximum and has a drop of more than 70 meters. Its water rushes down from a three-tiered cliff with tremendous force, with an average an-nual volume of flow of 50 cubic meters/second. Three cascades fall down from high peaks, dash against solid rocks and explode into millions of tiny water beads. The fall is awe-inspiring, and its thunder is audible before it even comes into view. The changing seasons transform the natural scenery of the waterfall throughout the year. In spring, green grasses on the precipices and colorful flowers in full bloom add a multicolored border round the waterfall; in autumn, the terraced fields around the waterfall turn golden yellow, the hills are crimsoned through and the mist of the hanging waterfall goes up to the sky; in autumn, the waterfall's clear water drops slowly, with sparkling water beads scattered here and there in the wind; and in summer, the waters of the fall cascade with the momentum force of an avalanche like ten thousand horses galloping ahead, presenting the most magnificent scene. The Detian Scenic Zone has enjoyed a reputation of being the "100-mile gallery," because its karst caves, rural scenery, deep and secluded valleys, broken cliffs and dangerous paths, smooth lakes rising in the narrow gorge, and local ethnic customs are like a number of Chinese ink and wash.

Danxia Landforms of China

中国丹霞概述

What is Danxia landform? So long as a person pays a visit to Danxia Mountain in Guangdong, one will immediately understand what Danxia landform is. Danxia landform is formed by red terrestrial sandstones and conglomerates after collapse and erosion, characterized by red rock walls and cliffs. A long time ago, human beings discovered that Danxia Mountain is totally different from other mountains. In the 1930s, Professor Chen Guoda, a famous Chinese geologist and a senior member of the Chinese Academy of Sciences, made a profound research on the redstone mountains in South China. In the name of the most typical Danxia Mountain, he named such landforms "Danxia landform," which was accepted by the academic community soon afterwards. The "Danxia landform" has gradually become a technical term of the world geography.

Thanks to the great efforts of the Chinese geologists in the past century, China has discovered 715 Danxia landforms according to the statistics by Mr. Huang Jin, an expert in Danxia geomorphology. Danxian Mountain has become a research base of the Chinese Danxia landforms.

Danxia Mountain – the Red Stone Park of China

丹霞山——中国的红石公园

Danxia Mountain, commonly known as "China's Red Stone Park," is about eight kilometers south of the seat of Renhua County, and 45 kilometers north of Shaoguan City, Guangdong Province in southeast China. In ancient times, the area was a huge lake. About 20 million years ago, intermittent uplift movements of the earth's crust made the lake water flow away and changed the area into a very beautiful landscape consisting of sheer precipices, overhanging rocks and craggy hills. As the sediments at the bottom of the lake are composed of red sandstones, the mountain is in red color, looking like multi-layer red rosy clouds, hence the name Danxia (Rosy Clouds) Mountain. Though the mountain is similar with the karst terrain, it does not consist of limestone. In geography, it is called "Danxia Landform."

With an area of 280 square kilometers, the Danxia Mountain Scenic Zone is just like a huge red-stone sculptures park, composed of undulating mountains, a forest of tall and steep peaks, and red rock walls and cliffs. The

Jinjiang River, the largest river in Renhua County, runs through Danxia Mountain, and winds through the peaks, forming a wonderful scenic marvel. Danxia Mountain is over 400 meters above sea level. Looking from a distance, the shapes of the three towering peaks are undulating and changeable, like a dragon or a boat. Climbing the mountain from the "dragon's tail," visitors will find Precious Pearl Peak on the left, Conch Peak in the middle and Old Monk Peak in the front, of which Conch Peak is the most majestic and precipitous, piercing into the sky. It is very easy to find different types of landforms in Danxia Mountain, which are the masterpieces created by nature. Now Danxia Mountain is a famous tourist attraction in China.

✻   ✻   ✻   ✻   ✻   ✻   ✻   ✻

Wuyi Mountain – a Typical Danxia Landform in China

武夷山——中国典型的丹霞地貌

Fifteen kilometers south of Wuyi City in Fujian Province in southeast China, Wuyi Mountain is a famous scenic zone in China, with an area of 60 square kilometers. Wuyi Mountain is isolated from the outside world by streams and ravines, and is known as the "No. 1 scenic wonder in southeast China." The elevation of the mountain is 1,000 to 1,100 meters, and Huanggang Mountain, the highest peak, is 2,158 meters above sea level. Its main tourist attractions include the Nine-Bend Stream, 36 peaks and 99 rocks. The meandering and green Nine-Bend Stream is flanked by numerous rock peaks composed of red sandstones, showing the typical Danxia landform. Numerous exquisite and gorgeous peaks in various shapes raise straight from the ground, adding radiance and beauty to the picturesque scenery of lakes and mountains and presenting a natural scenic wonder of green

waters and red mountains.

Great King Peak 大王峰, also called the Heavenly Pillar Peak, stands by the outlet of the Nine-Bend Stream, with an elevation of 536 meters. It is the first peak that tourists will see when entering Wuyi Mountain. At the peak's top, tourists can have a panoramic view

of all the 36 peaks in Wuyi Mountain.

Nine-Bend Stream 九曲溪, originates from Sanbao Mountain, and enters Wuyi Mountain via the Star Village. Then it winds about 7.5 kilometers in the mountain, with a total of nine bends. Today tourists can travel down the stream on bamboo raft excursions to appreciate the oddly shaped peaks on both banks of the stream, one of the best scenic sights in Wuyi Mountain. It takes only half a day for tourists to drift along the stream.

Heavenly Tour Peak 天游峰，is the main peak, 409 meters above sea level. It protrudes from the peaks around, which is often encircled by clouds and mist. Standing at the mountaintop, tourists can appreciate seas of clouds, just like taking a tour in Heaven, hence the name.

Jade Maiden Peak 玉女峰, to the south of the Second Bend Stream, is lofty and straight, in the shape of a girl with wild flowers on her hair, hence the name.

Wuyi Mountain has been included in the World Heritage List by the UNESCO.

① Great King Peak ③ Heavenly Tour Peak
② Nine-Bend Stream ④ Jade Maiden Peak

✳   ✳   ✳   ✳   ✳   ✳   ✳   ✳

Langshan Mountain
– a Danxia Landform with Green Peaks and Red Rock Walls

崀山——青峰赤壁的丹霞地貌

Situated in Xinning County, Hunan Province in central China, Langshan Mountain covers an area of 108 square kilometers and features a well-developed Danxia landform. The Fuyi River runs through the mountain, where peaks, rocks and waters are compactly laid out. Looking from a distance, tourists will find clusters of red peaks are undulating, rising one higher than another. A forest of red peaks presents a fantastic view. Most of the mountaintops are in round and arc shapes, covered with dark green primitive secondary forests. General Rock, 150 meters high, stands by the Fuyi River, like a general in a suit of armor guarding this miraculous land. Tiansheng Bridge in Mishai Village, 64 meters long, 14 meters wide and five meters thick, shows uncanny workmanship, making visitors gasp in admiration. Other tourist attractions include Pepper Peak, Camel Peak, the Whale Makes Havoc in the Sea and No. 1 Alley on Earth, each showing its own characteristics. The Fuyi River, which is as level as a mirror, is encircled by weeping willows and green bamboo on the banks, full of poetic beauty. Ai Qing, a famous modern poet, wrote an inscription after a visit to Langshan Mountain, reading: "Guilin boasts the most beautiful scenery on earth, but the landscape of Langshan Mountain is even more beautiful than Guilin."

Danxia Landforms of China

Zhangye Danxia Mountain
– a Palace in the Desert

张掖丹霞地貌——荒漠上的殿堂

Located in Daleba Gorge and Ice Gorge of Kangle Township in Shunan County, Zhangye City, Gansu Province, the Danxia landform is called Zhangye Danxia. In the arid area in west China, the Danxia landform here is totally different from those in south China as it does not grow vegetations and trees, making people feel desolate. Zhangye Danxia Mountain is in the shape of a palace, with lots of doors and windows around. Under the bright sunshine, the red mountain looks more fantastic and magnificent. Geologists call such Danxia landforms the "window-type and palace-type Danxia." According to the opinions of the experts, this type of Danxia landform can only be found in the arid areas, such as Gansu and Qinghai. In the surrounding areas lie groups of colorful hills, which are like waves undulating on the vast land, presenting a majestic and dynamic picture rarely seen in China.

Chinese Deserts

中国沙漠概述

The deserts are mainly distributed in northwest China. Dunes, sand lakes and oases are the main scenic spots in the desert. After constant contacts with the deserts, human beings have realized that only if we treat the desert well, can we survive on earth. China has a serious lesson that excessive reclamation and grazing made the country ruthlessly punished by nature. When spring was changing into summer, the northwestern regions of China, including Beijing, were subject to the sandstorm time and again, with a visibility of only three meters. Putting sands under control, planting trees and letting cultivated land revert to woodland are the basic national policy of China. China has created many miracles in the control of sands by mankind in the great project of fixing sands, planting trees and controlling sands, and has been well known as an example of the harmonious coexistence between mankind and the desert.

Deserts

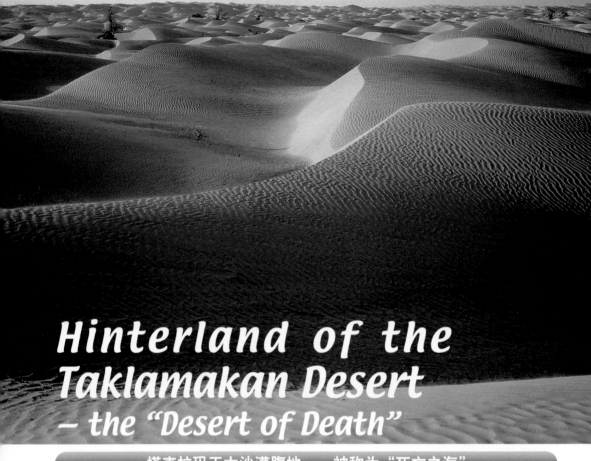

Hinterland of the Taklamakan Desert
– the "Desert of Death"

塔克拉玛干大沙漠腹地——被称为"死亡之海"

Located in the center of the Tarim Basin in the southern part of the Xinjiang Uygur Autonomous Region in northwest China, the Taklamakan Desert is about 300 kilometers from Hetian City in Xinjiang. It is the largest desert in China and the second largest in the world. The boundless stretch of desert contains various huge dunes in different shapes, such as pyramid-, dome-, scale-, feather- and earthworm-shaped dunes, presenting almost all the scenic wonders in the deserts all over the world. In the hinterland of the Taklamakan, there are several rivers, such as the Ketian, Keriya and Niya rivers, some of which are still running and the others have run dry, leaving the zigzagging green corridors in the vast desert, which are the scenic wonders in the desert.

In the past, the Taklamakan was known as the "Desert of Death" and the "Place of No Return," which has become history. Now the Taklamakan is run through by a highway, and oilfields were discovered in the vast desert. It proves that people can survive in the desert, and the desert can create wealth. It is another miracle in the desert.

The Badin Jaran Desert with the Highest Dune in the world

巴林吉林沙漠腹地——世界上最高的沙丘在这里

Located in the west of the Alxa Plateau in the Alxa League of the Inner Mongolia Autonomous Region in northwest China, the Badin Jaran Desert is the third largest desert in China, with a total area of about 44,000 square meters, and an average elevation of 1,300 meters. The flowing sand dunes make up 83 percent of the total area of the desert. The area around the Badin Jaran Temple, about 80 kilometers north of the Alxa Right Banner, is the hinterland of the Badin Jaran Desert, which presents the most fascinating scenery.

The Badin Jaran Desert is well known in the world for the height of the dunes (The relative altitude is between 200 and 300 meters). The dunes raise one higher than another in the desert, and Wuzhumu Sand Mountain is known as the "Sand King in the World," with an elevation of 528 meters. More than 140 lakes (called "Haizi" by the local people) in various sizes are spread between the numerous dunes on the vast desert, and most of them are salt lakes. Of them, the largest covers an area of 1.5 square meters. Around the lakes are marshlands and meadows, which are the important grazing grounds in the desert. The vast desert, large and tall dunes, silent lakes and slowly walking camels are the scenic wonders in the desert.

Humming Sandy Mountain and Crescent-Moon Spring
– the Sandy Mountain Always Accompanies the Limpid Spring

鸣沙山·月牙泉——沙漠与泉水互不侵犯

Known as the Divine Sand Mountain in ancient China, the Humming Sandy Mountain is five kilometers south of Dunhuang in Gansu Province, 40 kilometers from east to west, 20

kilometers from south to north and several dozen meters high. The sand peaks are steep and precipitous, looking like a knife. Standing at the top of the Humming Sandy Mountain, you will have a panoramic view of a forest of dunes and a limpid spring. You may be fascinated by an interesting practice as slipping downhill which can induce a sonorous thunder of the sand. According to historical records, when it is fine and the wind rests, the sand may play special music sounding like the orchestral music, hence the name "Sandy Mountain Sings as It Is Fine," which is a scenic wonder in Dunhuang. Legend has it that in ancient China, a general led his army to station here. One night when the wind howled, and yellow sands shut out the sky, the whole army was overwhelmed. At this moment, a sound of drums and a bugle was heard, hence the name the Humming Sandy Mountain.

The Crescent Spring lies at the northern foot of the Humming Sandy Mountain. In the shape of a crescent, the spring lushly grows float grasses and has so clear water that one can see to the bottom. Surrounded by sandy hills, the spring always has limpid water. When the wind blows, sands never drop into the spring. The moving sandy hills that always take the clear spring as their shadow is a scenic wonder indeed.

Shapotou – an Example of the Harmonious Coexistence Between Man and Nature

沙坡头——人与沙漠和谐相处的典范

Situated at the southeastern rim of the Tengger Desert, over 10 kilometers west of Zhongwei City in the Ningxia Hui Autonomous Region in northwest China, Shapotou is only about 30 meters from the northern bank of the Yellow River. By the riverbank, there is a large sand embankment, about 2,000 meters wide and 100 meters high, hence the name Shapotou (Sand Slope Head). It means that on the northern bank of the Yellow River is the Tengger Desert, and on the southern bank is the famous Loess Plateau. Thanks to the outstanding achievements in fixing sands and controlling sands by the Chinese people, the vast sea of yellow sands has been covered by a wide green forest belt, presenting a natural scenic wonder consisting of the desert, the long river, the high mountain and the oasis — an example of the harmonious coexistence between man and nature. The Chinese experts in the sand control have created a miracle that trains have run along the Baotou-Lanzhou Railway and gone through the desert for several dozens of years, a fact which has attracted many Chinese and foreign experts and scholars to come here to make investigations. Accordingly, Shapotou enjoys a high reputation in the world. Here tourists can ride camels to appreciate the sea of sands, take a sand bath, and do sand surfing. Further south lies the turbulent Yellow River. Tourists can take the tourist program of cruising the river aboard goat-skin dinghies.

Yardan Land-forms of China

中国雅丹概述

China's Yardan landforms are mainly distributed in the Xinjiang Uygur Autonomous Region, Qinghai and Gansu. Yardan landforms, deserts, salt deserts and mud deserts all belong to wilderness, but each has its own geological structure. Yardan landform was first discovered in the area around the Lop Nur Lake in Xinjiang in the early 20th century, when some Chinese and foreign experts made an investigation in Xinjiang, finding a large area of steep mounds, called "dangerously steep and precipitous hillocks" in the Uygur language, which was later translated into English as "Yardan." Yardan refers to the "wind-eroded" landform in the dry area consisting of wind-eroded mounds and depressions (ditches and troughs). In a desert, the strong wind is cruel, but without the strong wind, the wonderful Yardan landforms would not be formed. Hence the wind is named architect in the desert.

Yardan

Karamay Yardan Landform
– Known as the "Ghost City"

Situated in Wuerhe Area (also known as the Wuerhe Wind City) about 100 kilometers north of Karamay of Xinjiang in northwest China, the "Ghost City" is called the Yardan landform in geography. According to the research by geologists, it is the ruins of the geological phenomena of the Permian period in the Palaeozoic era. Over the vast horizon, there are a great number of wind-eroded mountains and city walls. Some mounds look like castles; and the others resemble lions, tigers and beasts, presenting a marvelous natural phenomenon. In the deep valleys, there are stone gourds and mushrooms, showing uncanny workmanship. In the daytime, the "Ghost City" is covered with mist, and filled with a deathly silence. At night when the strong wind comes, there is sad and shrill sound, like ghosts wailing and wolves howling, making people shiver all over, hence the name the "Ghost City."

Lop Nur Yardan Landform
– a Wind-eroded Scenic Wonder

罗布泊雅丹地貌——风蚀的奇观

Located in the Lop Nur area in the north of Ruoqiang County, Xinjiang in northwest China, Lop Nur has a clay stratum. The long-lasting erosion by torrential currents and strong winds has given birth to parallel "ridges" and "ditches" that cover a large area. The length of the "ridges" and "ditches" varies from several dozen meters to several hundred meters, and they are in different shapes, presenting wonderful scenery. The most typi-cal is the "Dragon City" in the northeast of Lop Nur, where the mounds have very hard salt crusts, 10 to 20 meters high and 200 to 500 meters long, looking like a number of dragons lying on the ground. Such a scene is rare in the world. The most interesting is that wild hemp and red willows grow in the Yardan landform, and sometimes you may see run-ning Mongolian gazelles and wild camels. All of these will give surprises to adventurers.

Chinese Caves

中国洞穴概述

Caves in China are mainly divided into two types: karst caves and non-karst caves. Guilin in south China boasts the most typical karst landform. Thrust up by the movement of the earth's crust, the limestone layers in Guilin were carved by wind and water into the oddly shaped hills and stone forests, in addition to an underground world consisting of karst caves, karst crevices and underground rivers.

China is a kingdom of caves in the world. According to the estimation by experts, China has nearly 10,000 caves in total, including about 1,000 karst caves that have been investigated, and nearly 400 karst caves that have been developed as tourist attractions. It is still a riddle that how many underground karst caves China actually has. Accordingly, we can only give a brief introduction to some major tourism karst caves as follows:

Caves

Zhijin Cave – "No. 1 Cave on Earth" in the Eyes of the Chinese People

织金洞——中国人心目中的"天下第一洞"

Zhijin Cave is about 23 kilometers north-east of the seat of Zhijin County of Guizhou Province in southwest China. The cave mouth is halfway up the mountain, about 15 meters high and 20 meters wide. It is a dry karst cave with a high elevation. At present, the section that has been exploited is 12.1 kilometers long, and 150 meters high and 75 meters wide at maximum. In general, the cave is about 60 to 100 meters high and wide, and covers a total area of over 700,000 square meters. Thanks to the complicated structure of strata and the unique karst landforms, the cave holds intermittent ponds, underground lakes, numerous stones that appear like monks, arhats, shepherds, jade bamboo shoots, curtains, flowers, trees, golden rats, sleeping lions, heavenly chickens, silver basins, and pagodas, and some precious stones, such as heligmites (helictite),

calcites, chrysanthemum stones, chicken blood stones and snakeskin stones. The sights inside the cave are indeed spectacular with rock formations of almost all conceivable kinds. A total of 47 galleries in Zhijin Cave have been exploited, and the largest one has an area of over 3,000 square meters. The maze-like galleries gather all kinds of karst wonders, including 120 stalactites, a rare scene in the world. In the Preaching Hall, a Buddha sits on a pagoda, which is over 20 meters high, preaching sutras to a large number of arhats. Some arhats hold the sutra; some listen to the lecture with great attention, or lower their heads in silent thinking; and the others exchange views with each other. They are of such a great variety of shapes and postures that none resembles another. The Snow Fragrance Palace is over 300 meters long, with an area of over 600 square meters. It is a white world, with crystalline ice pillars, transparent curtains and a vast expanse of snow, presenting picturesque scenery of north China. In addition, Zhijin Cave also boasts pearl fields, plum blossom fields, rice seedling fields and green bamboos swaying in the wind. In the eyes of the Chinese people, Zhijin Cave is the "No. 1 Cave on Earth," and is named the "Wonder on a Planet" by Chinese and foreign experts.

Furong Cave – an "Underground Art Palace"

芙蓉洞——被称为 "地下艺术宫殿"

By the Furong River in Jiangkou Town of Wulong County, Chongqing in southwest China, Furong Cave was discovered in May 1993 and was named the "world-level wonder and the first-class scenic cave."

Furong Cave, which is 2,700 meters long and has an area of 37,000 square meters, includes five scenic attractions: "Coral Jasper Lake," "Huge Curtain and Hanging Waterfalls," "Source of Life," "King of Stone Flowers," and "Dogtooth-like Crystalline Calcite Flowers." The "Coral Jasper Lake" covers an area of 32 square, and the calcite crystalline flowers by the lake are glittering

and translucent under the colorful light. Two jade-like stone bamboo shoots among the limestone flowers are exquisite and beautiful, looking like two graceful fairy maidens in a distance. According to the opinions of experts, Furong Cave is one of the largest and most beautiful pond speleothem sights in the world. As one of the famous scenic wonders in Furong Cave, the "Source of Life" is well known for stone bamboo shoots, 120 cm long and 124 cm in circumference, which are rare in the world.

In 2001, a scientific investigation by a multinational cave prospecting team discovered a secret in Furong Cave: In an area of 10 square kilometers around Furong Cave, there are 108 vertical wells, which are all linked with Furong Cave. Of them, Qikeng Cave is 920 meters deep, ranking first in China. According to statistics, Furong Cave contains over 100 varieties of speleothems, which are rare in China in terms of the quantity, beautiful shapes, purified quality and wide distribution. Hence Furong Cave is known as the "Underground Art Palace," and the "Cave Science Museum."

Huanglong Cave – a Karst Cave Known for Its Density of Stone Bamboo Shoots

黄龙洞——石笋最密集的溶洞

Situated in Hekou Village of Suoxiyu Town, five kilometers east of Wulingyuan District of Zhangjiajie City, Hunan Province in central China, Huanglong Cave was open to the public in 1984, with an area of about 100,000 square meters. Its total length is 7,640 meters, and its vertical height is 140 meters. With two layers of dry caves and two layers of water caves, Huanglong Cave contains one reservoir, two rivers, three ponds, four waterfalls, 13 halls, 98 corridors, nearly 1,000 jade-like ponds and about 10,000 stalactite peaks. The whole cave is just like a huge ancient tree with twisted roots and gnarled branches, caves contained in caves, rang upon rang of hills and meandering streams. The sights in the cave are very spectacular, with rock formations of almost all conceivable kinds. The most fascinating scenic sight in the cave is a forest of stone bamboo shoots, rank-

ing first in the density of stone bamboo shoots in the country. Of them, the "Mystical Needle for Calming Sea" is a rare sight in the country.

＊　＊　＊　＊　＊　＊　＊　＊

Tenglong Cave – the Largest Karst Tourist Cave in China

腾龙洞——中国最大的旅游溶洞

Located in the southeastern suburbs of Lichuan City, Hubei Province in central China, the entrance to Tenglong Cave is large and long, looking like a dancing dragon from a distance, hence the name Tenglong (Soaring Dragon) Cave. The cave mouth is 74 meters high, 64 meters wide, and 235 meters high at maximum. According to the preliminary verification, the total length of Tenglong Cave is 52.8 kilometers, being one of the largest karst caves that China has discovered so far.

With an area of over 200 square meters, Tenglong Cave can hold all the citizens of Lichuan City, totaling 830,000, three square meters per person on average. Tenglong Cave contains five peaks, 10 halls, and over 10 underground waterfalls, with hills contained in caves, and caves hidden in hills. The dry caves are linked with water caves; and large ones are connected with small ones. The rock formations in the cave are of all kinds of shapes and postures, mysterious and fascinating. The waterfall at the cave mouth, called "Crouching Dragon Swallowing the River," is over 50 meters wide, with a descent of over 30 meters. When the waterfall drops down, it gives out the thundering sound, and then flows into underground for 16.8 kilometers. The

lakes in Tenglong Cave are covered with mist; the Dragon Palace is deep, serene and supernatural; the underground wells are crystalline and dazzling; stone pagodas are in all shapes; and stone curtains can be seen everywhere. In 1988, 25 Chinese and foreign experts spent 32 days making a field investigation of the cave, and finally they reached a conclusion: Tenglong Cave is the largest tourist cave China has exploited so far, and is one of the special-class caves in the world.

Chinese Lakes

中国湖泊概述

China is a land of many lakes. Over 130 lakes exceed 100 square kilometers each. Most of China's lakes are concentrated in the two areas: (1) The middle and lower reaches of the Yangtze River, such as Poyang Lake, Dongting Lake, Taihu Lake, Hongze Lake, and Chaohu Lake, which are five major freshwater lakes in China; and (2) Qinghai-Tibet Plateau, which has the largest cluster of plateau lakes in the world. Most of them are inland salt lakes, of which Qinghai Lake is the largest.

As all lakes have simple shapes, it is very difficult for us to find wonders from them. But lakes can be divided into plain lakes, plateau lakes, freshwater lakes, sand lakes, salt lakes, urban lakes and suburban lakes. From them, we can select the most peculiar and the most beautiful lakes with the most outstanding characteristics so as to find wonders.

Qinghai Lake – the Largest Salt Lake in China

About 180 kilometers west of Xining City in Qinghai Province in northwest China, Qinghai Lake covers an area of 4,200 square kilometers and is over 360 kilometers in circumference. The salt content in the lake water comes to 10 to 20 percent, and Qinghai Lake is the largest salt lake in China. In the lake there are five islets — Haixin Islet, Sand Islet, Bird Islet and Stone Islet, of which Bird Islet is the most magnificent.

Bird Islet is on the northwestern corner of Qinghai Lake, with an area of less than one square kilometers, which is home to tens of thousands of migratory birds. In April every year, over 10 types of migratory birds, such as bar-headed gooses, pallass gulls and brown-

headed gulls, from Yunnan and Guizhou in southwest China and the island countries on the Indian Ocean gather on the island. Hence the period from May to June is the best season to observe birds, when visitors can see numerous nests, colorful bird eggs, and a great number of birds fly in the skies to blot out the sky and the sun, a scenic wonder indeed.

During a trip to Qinghai Lake, tourists can visit the Tibetan herdsmen's home, roam around the grasslands, high mountains, lakes and gobi deserts, ride camels, Tibetan horses and yaks, which are known as the boats on the plateau, watch the sunrise and appreciate the picturesque scenery.

Nam Co Lake – the Salt Lake with the Highest Elevation in the World

Located in southwest China, about 230 kilometers northwest of Lhasa in Tibet, Nam Co Lake covers an area of 1,940 square kilometers, and is over 33 meters deep, with an elevation of 4,718 meters. It is a salt lake with the highest elevation in the world. (Lake Titicaca, known as the "highest" lake in the world, is located in South America, with an elevation of 3,812 meters.)

In the Tibetan language, Nam Co means "Heavenly Lake." The lake water is blue, with the reflections of the snow-covered peaks, presenting a unique picturesque sight. The scientific research proves that Nam Co was

formed by the subsidence of the earth's crust and the activities of glaciers during the movement of the Himalayas in the Tertiary period. Five peninsulas stretch into Nam Co from different directions, of which the Zhaxi Peninsula is the largest, with an area of 10 square kilometers. The Zhaxi Peninsula, which is formed by reefs and a great number of karst caves, is the best place to appreciate the scenery of Nam Co. Jagged rocks of grotesque shapes and forests of peaks can be seen everywhere on the Zhaxi Peninsula. The forests of peaks are linked by natural bridges, presenting the rare natural scenic wonders on the Qinghai-Tibet Plateau. The most fascinating of Nam Co is clouds and chang-

ing lights. In one day, visitors can experience different climates and appreciate different scenery created by diverse light sources, making every visitor gasp in admiration. On the southern side of the lake stands the Nyainqentanglha Mountains, which is covered with white snow all the year round, with an elevation of 7,111 meters. When spring comes, groups of wild ducks fly to the islets to lay eggs and hatch baby ducks, adding vigor and life to the lake.

The Tibetan people regard Nam Co as the symbol of good luck and a peaceful life, and cherish deep love and many illusions for the Heavenly Lake. From May to September every year, many Buddhist believers go to the sacred lake to pay homage to Buddha. They measure every inch of the lakeside land by their footsteps or bodies to pray for happiness brought about by Buddha.

Heavenly Pond in the Changbai Mountains
– a Volcano Crater

长白山天池——火山喷出的天池

　　Located at the top of the main peak of the Changbai Mountains in Jilin Province in northeast China, the Heavenly Pond is a typical mountain lake, with an elevation of 2,194

meters. In the remote antiquity, the Changbai Mountains was a volcano. After the volcano had burst out a great amount of lava, a basin was left at the crater. With the passage of time, a lake appeared, and lava materials piled up around the crater later became 16 oddly shaped peaks encircling the lake. As the lake sits at the mountaintop and the water surface is 2,150 meters above sea level, it was named Heavenly Pond. The basin-shaped Heavenly Pond covers an area of 9.8 square kilometers; the average depth is 204 meters; and the deep-est spot reaches 312.7 meters. The temperature of the lake water is fairly low, and the lake freezes over six months a year. The Heavenly Pond is always covered by mist, and it is fine only a few days in a year. If the wind force is five, the waves on the lake will reach over one meter high. If it is fine, the pond is as smooth as a mirror, with the reflections of the precipices on the water surface, showing a scenic wonder of the Heavenly Pond.

Sand Lake – a Scenic Wonder in the Vast Desert

沙湖——大漠中的奇观

About 50 kilometers northwest of Yinchuan City in the Ningxia Hui Autonomous Region in northwest China, the Sand Lake is naturally formed by the floods from Helan Mountain over the years. The Lake borders the sloping fields of Helan Mountain in the west, and the undulating sand hills in the south, with an area of 22.42 square kilometers and an average depth of 2.2 meters. It is a special scenic zone featuring the scenery of the vast desert and the landscapes of the land of water in south China. In the shape of a crescent, the

Lake lushly grows reeds. When riding a boat on the lake, one will feel as if one entered a dense forest that blocks the sky and the sun. In the peninsula on the northern bank, tourists can ascend a height to observe numerous birds flying; in the western part of the lake, a vast area of lotus flowers vie with each other for glamour; and to the south of the lake lie sand hills, where visitors can do sand surfing, or ride camels to travel among sand hills and appreciate the scenery of the desert. The Mid-lake Bird Island covers an area about 10,000 square meters, which is home to hundreds of thousands of migratory birds. The unique picturesque scenery of the Sand Lake consists of limpid water, golden sands, reed, flying birds, swimming fish, beautiful lotus flowers and tall mountains in the distance.

* * * * * * * *

West Lake in Hangzhou
– a Place with Poetic Charm

杭州西湖——诗情与画意的地方

The lake is located in the west of the city proper of Hangzhou in east China, hence the name West Lake. The lake is skirted by rolling wooded hills on three sides and faces the city on one side. In the shape of an ellipsoid, West Lake covers an area of 6.03 square kilometers, of which the water surface comes to 5.66 square kilometers. The lake is 15 kilometers in circumference. The bottom of the lake is flat, and it is 1.5 meters deep on average. On the lake there are Bai and Su causeways. West Lake is divided into five small lakes, i.e., Outer, Inner, Yu, Sili and Lesser South lakes. In the lake, there are four

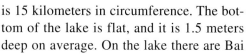

islets, namely, Solitary Hill, Lesser Yingzhou, Mid-lake Pavilion and Ruangong Islet. In the scenic zone with West Lake as the center, there are over 40 main scenic spots and historical sites, and over 40 key cultural relics and historical sites. West Lake is surrounded by rising and falling mountains, lushly growing flowers and trees, tall peaks, oddly shaped rocks, secluded caves, deep valleys, and limpid springs, ponds and streams, which are strewn with kiosks, towers, waterside pavilions, pagodas and grottoes. West Lake boasts picturesque scenery of lakes and mountains.

In ancient China, West Lake was a shallow bay, which was linked with the Qiantang River. Later, the shallow bay was silted up and became a lake. After it had been continuously washed by running mountain springs, and dredged by the locals in the past many years, it became the most beautiful city lake in China.

China has many cities, and a great number of city lakes as well. However, no city in the whole country has such a picturesque lake with profound culture like Hangzhou. Since ancient times, there have been many legends, poems and well-turned phrases about lakes. But it is only West Lake that is always like a poem and a painting wherever and whenever you will appreciate it.

Kanas Lake – the Farthest Lake from the Sea

喀纳斯湖——离大海最远的美景

Located in Bu'erjin County in the north of Xinjiang in northwest China, Kanas Lake means "beautiful, fertile and mysterious" in the Tibetan language. With an elevation of 1,374 meters, the moon-shaped lake covers an area of about 40 square meters, about 10 times that of the Heavenly Pond in Xinjiang. It is about 25 kilometers from south to north, and 1.5 to three kilometers from east to west. It is 188 meters deep at maximum, being one of the deepest lakes in China.

Surrounded by tall mountains, Kanas Lake has clear-cut vertical natural scenery. Standing by the lake, tourists can have a panoramic view of the seven scenic belts of the Altay Mountains, i.e., the meadow and grassland belt, the alpine coniferous and broadleaf forest belt, the alpine coniferous forest belt, the subalpine meadow belt, the alpine meadow zone, the tundra soil zone and the ever-lasting ice-snow zone. In the area around the lake are dense forests, where Siberian red pines, firs, Chinese spruces and larches grow lushly, and which are home to a number of rare birds and animals under state protection, such as red deer, gluttons, argali, snow hares and

wood frogs. Hucho taimen, thin-scaled salmons, river cods, Siberian toothed breams and other cold water fishes can be found in the lake, which are rare in China.

If you take a trip to Kanas Lake in summer, you may appreciate the scenery of four seasons. The top of the Atlay Mountains is covered with white snow; the pine forests halfway up the mountains are green, presenting the mountain scenery in autumn; colorful flowers are in full bloom in the lower part of the mountains; and Kanas Lake is picturesque with blue waves.

*　　*　　*　　*　　*　　*　　*　　*

China's Death Sea – the *Clone of the "Death Sea in the Middle East"*

中国死海——"中东死海"的克隆

Located in the China Death Sea Tourism   and Holiday Resort in Daying County,

Suining City, Sichuan Province in southwest China, the Death Sea has now become a tourism and holiday resort integrating floating, on-water recreational activities, recuperation and health care.

About 150 million years ago, the plate movement of the earth separated the continent, and gave birth to an inland lake between Israel and Jordan, known as the "Death Sea in the Middle East." In the same era, because of the same reason, an ancient underground salt lake, a geological wonder, appeared in Daying County in China. The huge salt lake is buried 3,000 meters underground. A survey proves that the underground salt lake covers an area of 700 square kilometers, and the salt reserve reaches 4.2 billion tons, and the seawater content is as high as 22 to 25 percent, hence it is named "China's Death Sea." It is surprisingly similar with the "Death Sea in the Middle East." They were born in the same era; both are located at a latitude of 30°N.; and their seawater composition and salt content are almost the same. Every four kilograms of seawater contains one kilogram of salt, so that people can float on the water surface without difficulty.

In 2003, the China Death Sea Tourism and Holiday Resort in Daying County rose straight from the ground, and the Death Sea in China that had been sunk in sleep for over 100 million years woke up. With advanced technologies, the Death Sea Tourism and Holiday Resort fetched underground salty seawater to form an artificial salt lake with an area of 50,000 square meters. Here visitors will not only feel the mystical floating, but also enjoy the salt treatment and hot spring.

China's Seacoasts

中国海岸概述

China is a coastal country, and its coastlines stretch 32,000 kilometers long, including 18,000 continental coastlines and 14,000 island coastlines.

The seacoasts in China mainly fall into two types: sand coasts and rock coasts. China's sand coasts are very beautiful, so that most of them have been developed into tourist attractions. Rock coasts are mainly composed of huge and dangerous rocks. Due to the erosion by seawater for many years, the coastal rocks have become charming and colorful natural scenic sights. The seacoast is one of the places with the earliest human activities, so that the ecological environment has been seriously damaged. The unexploited coasts and the intact coasts cannot be found in China.

Yalong Bay – China's "Hawaii"

About 10 kilometers east of Sanya City, Hainan Province in southeast China, the Yalong Bay undulates eight kilometers, in the shape of a rising crescent. As a sand coast, Yalong Bay boasts fine and soft white sands, gentle beaches, blue and limpid seawater, bright sunshine, hot weather all the year round, wide coasts, tall and straight palm and coconut trees, lush bushes and arbors, and undulating lawns, forming a boundless green corridor. However, the most fascinating in the Yalong Bay is the charm, changes and momentum of the vast sea. The front of the Yalong Bay is strewn with five green islets, making viewers feel that though the sea is vast, it has the limit. When embracing the sea, people will feel much safer. A bird's-eye view of the Yalong Bay reveals that it is like a green jadeite inlaid on a green jade, being the most beautiful coast in China.

Yehliu in Taipei – a Work of Art Carved by Seawater

台北野柳——海水雕成的艺术品

As it looks like a huge green turtle in a distance, it is also called "Yehliu Turtle." Due to the orogenic movement of the earth, the sedimentary rocks buried deeply at the bottom of the sea went up to the sea surface to produce cuestas, and sea-eroded rocks and caves. After the erosion by wind, rain and waves for thousands of years, a forest of 180 rocks appeared, consisting of honeycomb rocks, bean curd rocks, ginger-shaped rocks and weathered windows, of which Queen's Head, Candle Rock, Breast Rock, Plum Blossom Rock and Fairy Maiden's Shoe are the most famous. Yehliu, a work of art carved by seawater, is rare in the world.

It is located in Yehliu Village, Wanli Township, Taipei County, Taiwan Province, hence the name. As a rock peninsula, Yehliu protrudes from the sea, about 1,700 meters long, 200 meters wide and 62 meters high.

Chengshantou – China's Cape of Good Hope

Located in the east of Longxudao Town of Rongcheng City, Shangdong Province in east China, Chengshantou is at the eastern end of the Shandong Peninsula, and faces the Republic of Korea across the sea. Chengshantou, which is skirted by the sea on three sides and is linked with the continent on one side, is the eastern end where the continent and sea meet. An old legend says that Chengshantou is the end of the earth, hence the name "China's Cape of Good Hope." Along the coast, steep

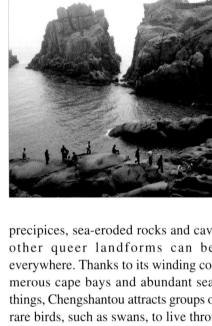

precipices, sea-eroded rocks and caves, and other queer landforms can be seen everywhere. Thanks to its winding coast, numerous cape bays and abundant sea living things, Chengshantou attracts groups of many rare birds, such as swans, to live through the winter every year — a scenic wonder along the Chinese coastal lines.

At the sea bottom near Chengshantou, reefs stand like a forest, and water swirls and runs swiftly. Waves are running high when the sea is calm and tranquil. A local saying goes: "Chengshantou, Chengshantou, nine boatmen of 10 are afraid of passing it." When the sea flies into rage, waves will go as high as over seven meters with great momentum, making viewers terrified and excited.

Qiantang River Tidal Bore
– a Scene of a Raging Sea

钱塘江潮——大海发怒的真容

At the mouth of the Qiantang River in the Hangzhou Bay, east of Hangzhou in Zhejiang Province in east China, the "Qiantang River tidal bore in autumn" is a natural wonder in the world. In the mid eighth lunar month every year, tides in the Qiantang River are roaring and rushing. During the period, the sun, earth and moon are basically on the same straight line; and the gravitational pull of the sun and moon are combined to produce high tides on the Qiantang River. When the soaring bore comes, it looks like a white thread from a distance; when it gets closer, it resembles thousands of horses running; and when it is before your eyes, the noise it generates sounds like thunder, with overwhelm-

ing momentum. The tide rolls in as high as a huge wall, with its crest reaching three to five meters, and dropping eight to nine meters. The rushing tide is great in strength and impetus, and soul stirring. The tide on the 18th day of the eighth lunar month every year, known as the "birthday of the Tide God," is the most magnificent. On the day, tens of thousands of people flock to Yanguan Town in Haining City to appreciate the scenic wonder in the world.

Changli Golden Coast
– a Wonder on the Dune Coast

昌黎黄金海岸——沙丘海岸上的奇观

Located in Changli County, about 300 kilometers east of Beijing in north China, the Changli Golden Coast was formed 2,000 to 3,000 years ago. The coast is covered with yellow sands, hence the name. A large dune belt that is parallel with the coast is more than 30 kilometers long and four kilometers wide. The dune rises up to a height of 44 meters at maximum, being the highest coastal dune in China. In the middle part of the Golden Coast there is a sand surfing ground. Tourists can go to the dune top by cable car, which is several dozen meters above the ground, and then slide down rapidly by sandboard, threatening but not dangerous. The coastline undulates over 50 kilometers, with fine and soft sand beaches, limpid seawater and an unruffled sea. In summer every year, the seawater bathing grounds are crowded with tourists.

The Changli Golden Coast is the highest and largest dune coast in China, featuring the combination of beach landforms and sand landforms, rarely seen in the world.

Victoria Bay – a Coastal Wonder Created by Mankind

维多利亚海湾——人类开发海岸的奇迹

Located between Hong Kong Island and the mainland of China, the Victoria Bay was named after Queen Victoria, as she was on the throne when the British troops occupied the harbor. In ancient times, it was the extension of the mountains. Due to the change of the crust, the fracture of the mountains and the invasion of seawater, the current bay was

formed. The Victoria Bay is about 10 kilometers from east to west, and 1.3 kilometers from south to north, and the water area is about 59 square kilometers. After the development and construction in the past 150 years, it has become an important harbor in the world. In the daytime or at night, the Victoria Bay illuminated by lights, which shows the perfection combination of skyscrapers and the sea, is an Oriental bright pearl on the Chinese coastlines, and a coastal wonder created by mankind.

Chinese Grasslands

中国草原概述

According to the estimation of experts, the grasslands in China make up about 40 percent of China's total territory. Whenever the grassland is mentioned, people will recite an ancient poem with a history of over 1,400 years as follows:

Below the Yinshan Mountains lies the Chile Prairie.
Over the earth hangs the sky like a huge yurt.
Between the vast sky and the boundless earth,
Flocks and herds appear as grasses bend to wind.

To look for the grassland wonders according to this poem is undoubtedly correct, but it is by no means the only criterion, because China has a vast territory, and various types of grasslands. For instance, in the frigid zone in west China, it is impossible for visitors to see the scene "Flocks and herds appear as grasses bend to wind," where grasses are short, but full of glamour.

Shall we include the grasslands in the book *Marvels of China*? We had been puzzled about the issue for quite a long time. But when we recalled our trips to the grasslands, we could not help thinking of the blue skies, white clouds, wild flowers, flocks of sheep, horses and cattle, yurts, mutton eaten with fingers, milk tea, bowed stringed instrument with a scroll carved like a horse's head, horserace, wrestling, archery, songs and dances on the grasslands. The grassland is open, colorful and beautiful; and the grassland culture is harmonious and selfless, which cannot be replaced by other ecologies.

Hulun Buir Eastern Grassland – the Most Beautiful Grassland

呼伦贝尔东部草原——最美的草原

Located in the east of Hulun Buir City of the Inner Mongolia Autonomous Region in north China, it is one of the famous grasslands in the world. With a flat terrain, the Hulun Buir Eastern Grassland embraces over 1,000 winding rivers, forming unique picturesque scenery. With high and dense grasses, the grassland is suitable for grazing horses and cattle. The famous sanhe cattle and sanhe horses were bred here. In summer, the grassland is a carpet of green grass, which is strewn with a multitude of blossoming flowers, flocks of cattle, sheep and horses, and yurts, being the most beautiful grassland in the eyes of the Chinese people. On July 10 every year, the Hulun Buir International Nadam Fair is solemnly held here, which attracts numerous domestic and foreign tourists. During the Nadam Fair, various kinds of sports competitions are held, such as the horserace, wrestling and archery.

Xilin Gol Grassland
– the Largest Grassland

the north, is the most typical grassland in the Xilin Gol Grassland.

Hequ Section of the Xilin River 锡林河河曲段 The Xilin River originates from Elun Lake in Hairqike Mountain in Hexigten Banner, Chifeng City, and stretches 270 kilometers long. When it makes a detour of Xilin Hot, it looks like a winding *katag* (white greeting scarves) on the vast grassland, presenting a beautiful scenic wonder on the grassland.

The Xilin Gol Grassland is located on the Xilin Gol Plateau in Inner Mongolia in north China. In the Mongolian language, "Xilin Gol" means the "river on the plateau." With an area of 200,000 square kilometers, the Xilin Gol has a smooth terrain, stretching as far as the eyes can see. The grassland is dotted with over 500 lakes and more than 20 winding rivers. The forage grasses grow well on the grassland, which is home to a great number of cattle, sheep and horses, as well as to numerous wild animals, such as swans, red-crested cranes, white cranes, black cranes, grassland vultures, Mongolian gazelles and other rare birds and beasts, forming many fascinating scenic pictures.

Ujimqin Grassland 乌珠穆沁草原, which is located on the way from West Ujimqin Banner to East Ujimqin Banner in

The Xilin Gol Grassland has been included in the International Man and Biosphere Reserve Network, and the Ujimqin Grassland and the Hequ Section of the Xilin River have become tourist attractions.

Ili Grassland – a Grassland with the Richest Landforms

伊犁草原——地形最丰富的草原

Located in Ili Prefecture in the Xinjiang Uygur Autonomous Region in northwest China, the Ili Grassland is distributed between Zhongtian Range of the Tianshan Mountains and the basin in the mountains. The fertile soil and a warm and moist climate are suitable for growing grasses. The Ili Grassland is undulating — now it appears on the mountaintop; now on the slopes; and now in the valleys. No one knows how many sub-grasslands are in the area. There are a wide variety of grasslands here, including the frigid grassy marshland, mountainous grassy marshland, mountainous grassland, desert grassland, valley grassy marshland, and so on, which form a symphonic music with the snow-capped mountains, forests and valleys in the surrounding areas. The four most famous grasslands in the Ili Grassland are: Nalaty, Gongnaisi, Zhaosu and Tangbula. The Kazak people are an ethnic group on horseback. They go out to graze sheep and cattle at sunrise, and come back at sunset day by day and year after year, freeing from care and enjoying the beautiful grassland bestowed by nature.

Nagqu Frigid Grassland
– the Highest Grassland

那曲高寒草原——最高的草原

Embraced by the Tanggula Mountains and the Nyainqentanglha Mountains in north Tibet, the Nagqu Frigid Grassland is a representative of China's frigid grassy marshlands, with an average elevation of over 4,200 meters. The vast Nagqu Grassland embraces many lakes scattered all over like stars in the sky, crisscrossed rivers and numerous geothermal hot springs. Over the boundless grassland, the dense grasses are only three to five cm high, but their roots are strong and resistant to low temperature. The divot is full of elasticity. Looking from a distance, it seems that the grassland was covered with a huge green carpet, which is strewn with flocks of sheep and cattle, forming a scenic wonder on the frigid plateau of Tibet.

Part Two Architectural Marvels of China

第二部分　中国建筑景观

China's long history of over 5,000 years has left numerous architectural heritages. When looking for the architectural marvels of China, we must understand the ancient Chinese people's unique cultural viewpoint and aesthetic standards. In ancient China, the people paid a great attention to the magnificence of architectural groups, rather than the height of a single building; and stressed the safety layout and auspicious decorations rather than abstract architectural shapes. For the design of architectural groups ranging from cities, imperial palaces to civilian residences, a cluster of architectural structures is often encircled by a wall, outside of which is a moat, thus forming a strict-precaution, isolated and self-sufficiency layout. Every architectural group has a core part, with a clear distinction between the primary and the secondary. Spaces are always reserved between architectural structures for building kiosks, pavilions, terraces and towers and growing flowers and trees. In this way, people can contact with nature, feel the changes in the four seasons, and understand the boundlessness of the universe without going out of the palace, garden and home, reflecting the perfect combination of man and nature.

The Great Wall

中国长城概述

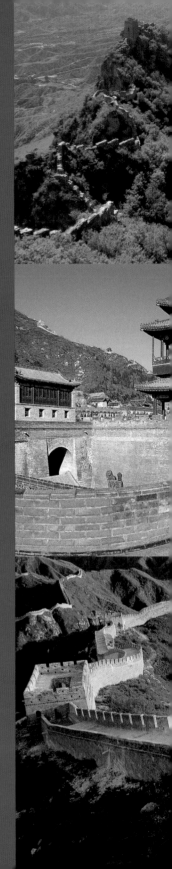

In the Spring and Autumn period (770-476 B.C.) and the Warring States period (475-221 B.C.), the states in north China built walls at the strategic places to defense with each other. In 221 B.C., when Qin Shihuang (First Emperor of the Qin Dynasty) conquered all the other six ducal states and unified China, he ordered to link up the walls built by the states of Qin, Zhao and Yan and extend them, so as to ward off the incursions of the Xiongnus (the nomadic people living in the north of China). Now the ruins of the walls built in the Qin Dynasty (221-207 B.C.) can still be seen. Reinforcement and renovations were carried out in the areas in north China that bordered the land inhabited by the nomadic people. In the Ming Dynasty (1368-1644), to resist the Dada, Waci and Nuzhen along the nation's borders, the Great Wall underwent major repairs and construction on 20

occasions. To ensure the efficient control of the defenses along the northern frontiers, the Ming authorities divided the entire Great Wall environs into nine zones and placed each under the control of a *zhen* (garrison headquarters). Two further garrison headquarters were added later. Thus the defense system ultimately consisted of eleven garrisons in nine zones, involving a total of over 97,660 officers and soldiers. The Great Wall stretches over 7,300 kilometers long, commonly known as the 10,000 *li* (one *li* = 0.5 kilometer) Great Wall.

The Great Wall mainly consists of the passes, beacon towers and walls. The most famous passes along the Great Wall are: Shanhai Pass in the east, Juyong Pass in Beijing and Jiayu Pass in the west.

The construction of the Great Wall was a huge project of the feudal dynasties in Chinese history. In many places, the slopes were very steep, making the construction very difficult. The transportation of stone slabs, bricks, lime and other construction materials to the mountains was an extremely arduous job. According to a rough estimation, the construction materials used for building the wall in the Ming Dynasty totaled 50 million cubic meters of bricks and stones, and 150 million cubic meters of earth. If we build a long wall, one meter wide and five meter high, with these bricks, stones and earth, the wall will be long enough to circle the earth for one time; and if we pave a road, which is five meters wide and 0.34 meter thick, the road can circle the earth for three times. The Great Wall is an important military defensive project in north China in ancient times, as well as one of the great projects in the world. The Great Wall is No. 1 wonder of China, and one of the commonly acknowledged wonders in the world. The Great Wall has been included in the World Heitage List by the UNESCO.

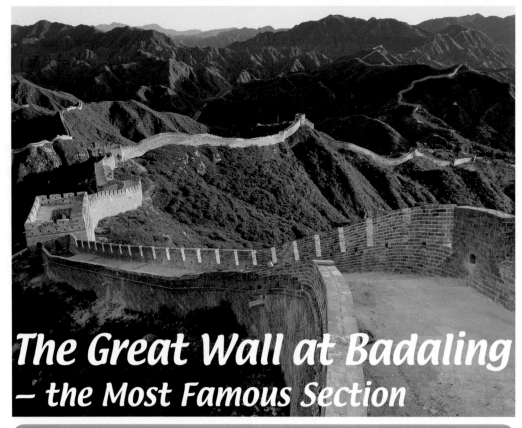

The Great Wall at Badaling
– the Most Famous Section

八达岭长城——最著名的一段长城

Located in Yanqing County in the northwestern suburbs of Beijing, about 60 kilometers from the city proper, the Great Wall at Badaling was first constructed in the 18th year of the Hongzhi reign period (1505) of the Ming Dynasty, being the most famous section of the Great Wall in China. The Wall at Badaling was built along the mountains, and the heights and widths vary. The average height is six to seven meters; and the average width is four to six meters. Five horses or 10 people can walk along it abreast. It is the most typical and most magnificent section built in the Ming Dynasty. The outside of the Wall is built with huge rectangular stone slabs; the inside is filled with earth and rocks; and the top of the Wall is paved with square bricks. The battlements have crenels, embrasures, peepholes and apertures for archers. To meet the needs of defense, watchtowers were built in at 300-meter intervals. There are two kinds of towers: the two-story watchtowers, and the wall towers. The top stories of the watchtowers were designed for observing enemy movement, with peep-holes, apertures for archers, and the equipment for giving smoke signals; the lower stories were used for storing grain, fodder, military equipment and gunpowder, as well as for quartering garrison soldiers. The wall towers built in the level and gentle places are in the same height with the Great Wall. On the wall towers there are houses for soldiers to be on sentry or on patrol. Badaling is over 800 meters above sea level. Standing at the peak, visitors can have a panoramic view of both sides of the Great Wall, which is like a long dragon lying on the undulating peaks, without the head and tail, powerful and magnificent.

* * * * * * * *

The Great Wall at Juyong-guan – the Most Complete Section

居庸关长城——最完整的一段长城

Located in Changping District in the northern suburbs of Beijing, Juyongguan is an important section of the Great Wall at Badaling, as well as a famous ancient military town, being the unique on the 10,000-*li* Great Wall. The Great Wall at Juyongguan is strategically situated and difficult of access, totaling 4,142 meters long. The Juyongguan Pass has the Cloud Platform, a government office, a warehouse, a library, an ammo warehouse, Confucian studies and other facilities, with rich cultural connotations, hence the name the "Museum of the Great Wall." In the Ming Dynasty, a place for sta-

tioning troops was set up here, so that 5,000 to 6,000 soldiers were stationed here all the year round. Accordingly it was an important defensive base of old Beijing.

*   *   *   *   *   *   *   *   *

The Great Wall at Simatai
– the Most Precipitous Section

司马台长城——最险峻的一段长城

Located in Miyun County in the northeastern suburbs of Beijing, about 140 kilometers from the city proper, the Great Wall at Simatai was a section meticulously built by Qi Jiguang, a famous general of the Ming Dynasty. This section was built on the mountain ridge, rising and falling on the cliffs and flanked by precipices, making viewers

tremble with fear. The main tourist attractions include Wangjing Tower, Fairy Maiden Tower, Heavenly Ladder, Heavenly Bridge, etc., of which Wangjing Tower is the highest, with an elevation of 986 meters. Standing at the tower, visitors can see Beijing in a distance on a fine day. The Great Wall at Simatai is 19 kilometers long, and includes 135 watchtowers. The well-conceived layout integrates all characteristics of the Great Wall, so that this section at Simatai "ranks first of China's Great Wall."

The Great Wall at Shanhaiguan – the Most Famous Section in Northeast China

山海关长城——中国东北最著名的一段长城

Located in northeast China, about 15 kilometers northeast of Qinhuangdao in Hebei Province, Shanhaiguan is an important pass in the eastern part of the Great Wall. As the pass is between a mountain and a sea, it is called "Shanhaiguan" (Mountain and Sea Pass). As the strategic passage between the north and northeast China, this pass has been a bone of contention for military strategists since the ancient times, known as "No. 1 Pass of the Great Wall."

The wall of Shanhaiguan Pass, built with bricks and stones, is 14 meters high, seven meters thick, and more than four kilometers in circumference. There are four city gates in the east, west, south and north, respectively. With the passage of time, only the tower of the East Gate now exists. On the gate-tower, a large horizontal inscribed board is hung, with five Chinese characters, meaning "No. 1 Pass Under Heaven." On the three sides of the tower, there are 68 windows for archers. Once you ascend the tower and take a broad view afar, you will see high mountains in the north, rising one higher than another, on which sits the undulating and magnificent Great Wall; and the section stretches along the eastern wall directly to the sea in the south, like a huge dragon diving into the sea to drink water, hence the name "Old Dragon's Head." The Old Dragon's Head, which is five kilometers south of Shanhaiguan Pass, is the starting point of the eastern section of the Great Wall built in the Ming Dynasty, about 10 meters high, with over 20 meters into the sea.

✳   ✳   ✳   ✳   ✳   ✳   ✳   ✳

The Great Wall at Jiayuguan – the Most Famous Section in Northwest China

嘉峪关长城——中国西北最著名的一段长城

Situated in the suburbs of Jiayuguan City, Gansu Province in northwest China, Jiayuguan Pass is at the western end of the Great Wall, and borders the Gobi Desert in the north, and the Qilian Mountains in the south. Known as the "No. 1 Strategic Pass Under Heaven," Jiayuguan Pass was an important communication center on the world-renowned Silk Road, and in ancient China, the economic and cultural exchanges between China and the Western countries must go through Jiayuguan Pass. Now it has the best-preserved gate-tower on the Great Wall. With an area of 335,000 square meters, the gate-tower is 11.7 meters high and 733 meters in circumference. On each of the four corners of the city wall stands a turret, which is in the shape of a fortress, very solid.

On both sides of the Great Wall, beacon towers (also known as "smoke mounds" in ancient China) were built at 2.5 to five-kilometer intervals to relay military information. At the approach of enemy troops, smoke signals gave the alarm from the beacon towers in the daytime and fires did this at night while guns were fired. It was a very effective communication form in ancient China. Legend has it that smoke signals made of wolf dung were thick and straight, and could send emergency signals to distant places. Hence the beacon tower is also called the "wolf smoke tower."

Chinese Palaces

中国宫殿概述

The palace was the place where the emperor held court and the imperial family lived. The Chinese palace represented the highest architectural level of the relevant era.

After the emperors of the past dynasties got the power, they would have new palaces built, which were usually located in the central part of the capital, reflecting the feudalist ideology of taking the emperor as the center. In general, an imperial palace is composed of the outer palace, where the emperors held official audiences, and the inner palace, which served as the living quarters for the imperial family. All the halls and rooms in the palace are independent, and are linked with each other, to ensure the safety of the emperors. Moreover, tight security and defensive measures were taken, such as building high walls around the palace and digging a wide moat.

Most of the capitals and palaces were destroyed in the war when past dynasties declined and the emperors were changed. The well-preserved palaces in China now include the former Imperial Palace in Beijing, the former Imperial Palace in Shenyang, the former Imperial Palace of the puppet state of Manzhoukuo in Changchun and the Potala Palace in Tibet. The former Imperial Palace in Beijing and the Potala Palace in Lhasa are the architectural wonders.

The Former Imperial Palace in Beijing – the Largest Palace in the World

北京故宫——世界上最大的皇宫

The former Imperial Palace, also known as the Forbidden City and the Palace Museum, is located at the center of Beijing. The construction of the Imperial Palace started in the fourth year of the Yongle reign period (1406) of the Ming Dynasty and was completed in the 18th year of the Yongle reign period (1420). With an area of 720,000 square meters, the Imperial Palace has 980 buildings with some 8,700 rooms, and is surrounded by walls, 10 meters high and three kilometers long. On the four corners of the walls stand turrets, and the walls is encircled by a moat 52 meters wide, showing ironclad defense. After the observation of the celestial body, the ancient Chinese astronomers discovered that the location of the Crape Myrtle Star in the hub of the Polaris remains unchanged forever, and is the center of the stars and constellations. Hence they named the place where the Heavenly Emperor lived the "Crape Myrtle Palace." The emperor in the feudal society believed that they "owned Heaven and earth," and his residence was the strongly fortified "forbidden area." Hence the people called the palace encircled by high walls where the emperors lived the "Forbidden City." It is also called the Palace Museum because it was where the emperors of the Ming and Qing dynasties resided and the Palace Museum is located.

❶

The Imperial Palace is composed of the outer palace and the inner palace. The outer palace mainly consists of the Hall of Supreme Harmony (Taihedian)太和殿, the Hall of Central Harmony (Zhonghedian)中和殿, and the Hall of Preserved Harmony (Baohedian) 保和殿, with the Hall of Cultural Brilliance (Wenhuadian)文华殿 and the Hall of Military Prowess (Wuyingdian)武英殿 on the two wings, where the emperors held grand ceremonies, received officials and exercised

Chinese Palaces

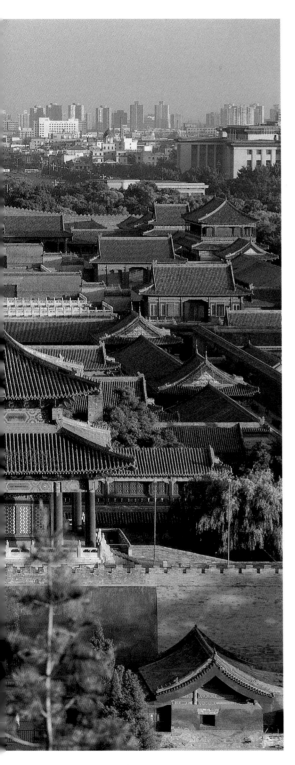

his rule over the state. The inner palace is mainly composed of the Palace of Heavenly Purity (Qianqinggong)乾清宫, the Hall of Union and Peace (Jiaotaidian)交泰殿, the Hall of Earthly Tranquility (Kunninggong)坤宁宫, and the six palaces on the eastern and western sides, respectively, where the emperors handled state affairs, and the imperial family lived, had entertainments and worshipped gods.

The Hall of Supreme Harmony 太和殿 is the most striking building in the outer palace, commonly known as "Hall of Golden Chimes," which was the ruling center of the emperors in the Ming and Qing dynasties, and where all the important ceremonies were held. The hall is 35.05 meters high, and about 63 meters wide and covers an area of 2,377 square meters. With red walls and yellow tiles, it is the widest, deepest and highest hall in the ancient architectural structures of China. The hall contains 72 pillars, including six gold-lacquered pillars carved with coiled dragons. Above the throne is a gilded coffered ceiling with a traditional design of dragons toying with pearls. The walls on the four sides are decorated with "gilded doors and windows," showing high craftsmanship. The roof decorations of nine kinds of beasts are also of the highest rank in the country. All

3

Marvels of China

Chinese Palaces ■

4

5

these designs fully display the emperor's "supreme" dignity.

On the terrace in front of the hall are a sundial in the east and a grain-measure in the west, indicating the emperor's concern for agriculture; and some bronze incense burners, tortoises and cranes, which were the utensils for burning pine and cypress branches and sandalwood when a ceremony was held, suggesting a peaceful and stable country. On the terrace, there are also two bronze cauldrons for storing water in case of fire.

The Hall of Central Harmony 中和殿 is behind the Hall of Supreme Harmony. With square eaves and a round roof, it contains beautiful carvings and colored drawings. This hall served as a resting place for the emperor on his way to the Hall of Supreme Harmony. He glanced over the memorials to the throne, and received members of the cabinet and officials before going to the Hall of Supreme

Harmony.

The Hall of Preserved Harmony 保和殿 stands behind the Hall of Central Harmony. In the Ming Dynasty, the emperor often changed his clothes here. In the Qing Dynasty, on the lunar New Year's Eve, the emperor gave banquets here to princes of vassal states and high-ranking officials. In the late years

of the Qianlong reign period, the emperor also supervised here the final stage of examinations to select officials from among scholars from all over the country. A central imperial ramp stands behind the Hall of Preserved Harmony. It is nearly 17 meters long, three meters wide, 1.7 meters thick and weighs more than 200 tons, carved with a dragon flying amid clouds. It is the largest stone carving preserved by China.

The Three Major Halls 三大殿 are the main buildings of the outer palace in the Imperial Palace. The Hall of the Supreme Harmony stands in the front; the Hall of Central Harmony is in the middle; and the Hall of Preserved Harmony is the last. The three halls sit on a terrace in the shape of a Chinese character "土" (meaning earth). The ancient theory of the five elements (metal, wood, water, fire and earth) believes that earth should be in the

of white marble, with a total of 1,488 pillars carved with clouds, dragons and phoenixes. In addition, 1,142 hornless dragonheads made of white stones are used to drain water. When it is raining, there will appear a scenic wonder of over 1,000 dragons spurting out water simultaneously. The three main halls surrounded by many small side rooms are majestic, presenting the most magnificent architectural complex in the Imperial Palace.

The Inner Palace 内廷 is behind the Hall of Preserved Hall. The inner palace, or the residential quarters of the imperial family, starts from the Gate of Heavenly Purity (Qianqingmen)乾清门. Along the central axial line stand the Palace of Heavenly Purity, Hall of Union and Peace, Hall of Earthly Tranquility and 12 courtyards. To the east and the west of the Palace of Heavenly Purity, there are six groups of courtyards, respectively. Each courtyard consists of the front and back halls and the small side rooms in the east and west.

The Imperial Garden 御花园 is situated at the northern end of the central axial

center, so that the terrace is in the shape of "土," symbolizing the three halls are the center of the country. The three halls stand on a three-tiered terrace surrounded by balustrades

9

line, with an area of about 11,700 square meters. The garden includes over 20 architectural structures in various sizes, which are exquisitely laid out, and is strewn with artificial hills, trees, ponds, flowers, potted landscapes and paths paved with colorful cobblestones. It is a beautiful imperial garden.

The Imperial Palace contains a great number of precious cultural relics, which are important data for the study of the history of the Ming and Qing dynasties, and the art of the past dynasties. In 1925, it was named the Palace Museum. After the founding of New China, large-scale renovations have been taken. Now the Palace Museum includes the Art Hall of the Past Dynasties, Treasures Hall, Hall of Paintings and Hall of Clocks and Watches.

The resplendent and magnificent Imperial Palace is the largest and best-preserved ancient palace architectural complex in the world, as well as a bright pearl with extraordinary splendor in the world ancient architecture warehouse. It has been included in the World Heritage List by the UNESCO.

① Palace of Heavenly Purity
② A full view of the Forbidden City
③ Hall of Supreme Hamony
④ Hall of Supreme Hamony
⑤ The bronze crane
⑥ Palace of Heavenly Purity
⑦ Hall of Central Harmony and Hall of Preserved Harmony
⑧ The Grain-Measure
⑨ Imperial Garden
⑩ The Golden Water Bridge and white marble balustrades in the Forbidden City, and the Meridian Gate in the distance

Potala Palace (the mid 17th century) – the Palace with the Highest Elevation in the World

布达拉宫（17世纪中叶）——世界上海拔最高的宫殿

Situated in Marpo Rill Hill (or Red Hill) in Lhasa, Tibet in southwest China, the Potala Palace is a famous castle-like architectural complex and an ancient architectural complex of the Tibetan people.

In the Sanskrit language, Potala means the "sacred land of Buddhism." In the seventh century, the emperor of the Tang Dynasty gave Princess Wencheng to Songzam Gambo, unifier of Tibet, in marriage. To welcome his bride, Songzam Gambo had a palace built here, which was later destroyed in the war. In the mid 17th century when the Fifth Dalai was in power, he had the White Palace built and then had the Red Palace expanded to the present scale.

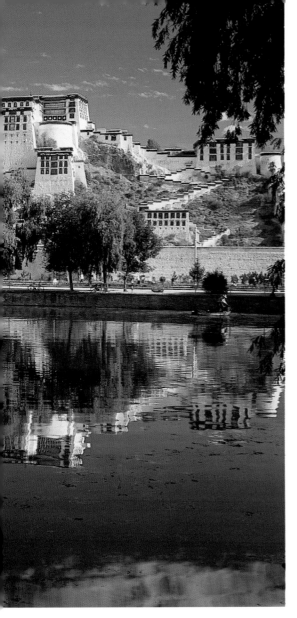

structures in the Potala were built on the cliffs, with row upon row of buildings, and all the roofs of the five palaces are covered with gold-gilded tiles. Here are eight stupas (dome-like mounds) containing the salt-dried and embalmed remains of most Dalai Lamas, of which the stupas of the Fifth and 13th Dalai Lamas are the highest, 14 meters high. These stupas, all the similar in shape but differing in size, are covered with gold leaf and studded with jade and precious stones. According to the records, the construction of the stupa of the Fifth Dalai Lama used 3,721 kilograms of gold and nearly 10,000 precious stones. In addition, the Potala also contains colorful murals that cover an area of over 2,500 square meters, nearly 1,000 Buddhist pagodas, 10,000 statues and *Tangkas* (唐卡) (traditional Tibetan paintings), *Pattra* leaves, *Kangyur* (the Tibetan Buddhist canon) and other rare treasures, in addition to the imperial edicts and gold seals given to Dalai Lamas by the emperors, a superb collection of exquisite and beautiful porcelain wares, jade and arts and crafts, which are all priceless. The Potala Palace integrates the Tibetan religion, politics, history and art; hence it is named the History Museum of Tibet. It has been included in the World Heritage List by the UNESCO.

With a total area of 130,000 square meters, the Potala Palace was the Winter Palace of Dalai Lamas of the past ages, and the ruling center of the integration of religion and politics in old Tibet. The 13-story main building is a stone-and-wood structure, 115.89 meters high and 400 meters long from east to west. The Potala includes the palaces, halls for worshipping Buddha, chanting halls, dormitories, stupas and courtyards. All the architectural

Chinese Cities

中国城市概述

　　The construction of the Chinese cities began 5,000 years ago at least, and the ancient Chinese cities generally fell into two types: capital cities and ordinary cities. The ancient capitals were all laid out with the imperial palace as the center, and civilian residences in the surrounding areas; and the ordinary cities took the local administration seats of the prefectures and counties at the core, with the temples and civilian residences in the nearby areas. It is the concrete reflection of the feudal hierarchy in the construction of the Chinese cities.

　　Now China has only seven well-preserved ancient cities, i.e., Xi'an, Nanjing, Jingzhou, Xiangyang, Xingcheng, Pingyao and Chongwu, of which Xi'an and Nanjing once served as the capital cities. In ancient China, building a city attached great importance to the military defense works. Usually, a city was encircled by high walls, which was bordered by a moat. The high city walls and wide moat were built for the safety of the city. Most of the old cities are square or rectangular; city gates were built on the four sides of the city walls; and on each city gate stood a majestic tower. In the daytime, the city gates were wide open; and at night they were all closed, making the people in the cities feel tranquil and safe. In the center of a city stood the Drum and Bell towers. In the morning, the bell was tolled; and at night the drum was beaten. In the city, the streets in the shape of "十"or chessboard were built. In the land of water in south China, the streets and lanes by waters are linked with the rivers outside of the city, with convenient transportation facilities by land and water. Now most of the ancient cities of the past dynasties have disappeared, leaving only some ruins. Only a small number of ancient cities that still exist are the city wonders of China. The new cities in China have sprung up like bamboo shoots after a spring rain throughout the country. This chapter also includes the Shanghai Pudong New Area; and we wish readers would accept it.

Tian'anmen Square in Beijing – the Largest Urban Square in the World

北京天安门广场——世界上最大的城市广场

Located in the city proper of Beijing, the Tian'anmen Square covers an area of 440,000 square meters and can accommodate one million people at the same time. As the largest square in the world, it attracts tens of thousands of visitors to take pictures everyday. In particular, many people are interested in watching the flag-raising ceremony in the morning and the flag-lowering ceremony at dusk.

Tian'anmen 天安门 is on the northern side of the Tian'anmen Square; and the Tian'anmen Gate-tower was originally the front gate of the Imperial Palace of the Ming and Qing dynasties. First constructed in the 15th year of the Yongle reign period (1417) of the Ming Dynasty, the gate, 34.7 meters high, sits on a meticulously carved Sumeru base made of white marbles, which is a red platform over 10 meters high. Right in the middle is hung a huge portrait of Mao Zedong, on both sides of which are two long slogans, reading: "Long Live the People's Republic of China!" and "Long Live the Great Unity of

2

3

the People All over the World!" On the red platform sits the resplendent and magnificent Tian'anmen Gate-tower, which has double and upturned eaves, carved beams, painted pillars, glazed tiles and red walls. The Gold Water River lies at the foot of the gate-tower, and five beautifully carved marble stone bridges, known as Gold Water bridges, span the Gold Water River. Two pairs of large stone lions and straight and exquisite carved ornamental columns match each other well, making the Tian'anmen Gate-tower become a complete architectural masterpiece. Tian'anmen is the symbol of New China. On October 1, 1949, Chairman Mao Zedong ascended the tower, and proclaimed the founding of the People's Republic of China to the world; the first red flag was raised; and over 300,000 citizens of Beijing gathered at the Tian'anmen Square to attend the solemn founding ceremony. The solemn and respectful Tian'anmen Square is a component part of the national emblem of China.

The Monument to the People's Heroes 人民英雄纪念碑 is in the center of the Tian'anmen Square, which was erected in accordance with a resolution at the First Plenary Session of the Chinese People's Political Consultative Conference to commemorate the heroes who laid down their lives in the people's revolutionary struggles over the 100 years. Construction began on August 1, 1952 and the monument was unveiled on May Day, 1958. The monument is 37.94 meters high from ground to top, and 3.24 meters higher than Tian'anmen, being the tallest monument in the Chinese history. On the front side is an inscription by the late Chairman Mao Zedong: "Eternal glory to the people's heroes!" The inscription on the south side was drafted by Chairman Mao Zedong and in the handwriting of the late Premier Zhou Enlai. Around

the lower plinth are eight large white marble reliefs and two smaller reliefs, totaling 40.68 meters long, which depict China's glorious history of the revolutionary struggles over the 100 years, and cite the eternal contributions of the people's heroes.

Chairman Mao's Memorial Hall 毛主席纪念堂 is situated at the southern end of the Tian'anmen Square, and construction was

6

finished on September 9, 1977. It is a square magnificent hall with the characteristics of the Chinese national style. The Memorial Hall consists of three main parts: North Lobby, Central Hall and South Lobby. The North Lobby is for the commemoration of the late Chairman Mao, with a white marble statue, three meters high, of Chairman Mao seated in an armchair in the center of the lobby. Behind the statue, a wood needle-pointed tapestry covers the back wall, depicting the vast landscape of China. In the Central Hall, the body of the late Chairman Mao lies in a state. Draped with the flag of the Communist Party of China, the body lies in a crystal coffin surrounded by colorful fresh flowers. Around the Chairman Mao's Memorial Hall grow various kinds of flowers, grasses and trees from all over the country.

The Great Hall of the People 人民大

会堂 is on the western side of the Tian'anmen Square. It was constructed in 1959, and now is the place where the National People's Congress convenes, and the state leaders and the Chinese people attend political and cultural activities. The eaves covered with glazed tiles in yellow and green colors, the tall corridor pillars, the huge hall, over 40 meters high, and the clear-cut architectural structures on all sides form a magnificent and splendid picture. Facing the Tian'anmen Square, the Great Hall of the People has a national emblem inlaid above the gate. Entering the Great Hall, visitors will see 12 high light gray marble stone door pillars, 25 meters high each, and the elegant and simple central lobby. Behind the central lobby is a large auditorium, 76 meters wide and 60 meters deep, which can hold 10,000 audiences. The Banquet Hall, in the north wing, can seat 5,000. The south wing

112

Marvels of China

Chinese Cities

contains the offices of the Standing Committee of the National People's Congress. The Great Hall of the People also contains the meeting halls, one for each province, municipality and autonomous region in China. Foreign guests are often entertained at banquets and receptions at the Great Hall of the People.

The Great Hall of the People in its entirety occupies 171,800 square meters, 206.5 meters from east to west, 336 meters from south to north and 46.5 meters at the highest. It is over 10 meters higher than Tian'anmen (34.7 meters), and is larger than the effective construction area of the whole Imperial Palace of the Ming and Qing dynasties (with an area of about 150,000 square meters). As a whole, the Great Hall of the People is more magnificent than Tian'anmen, proving that the Chinese people in the modern era are superior to their forefathers. However, the construction of the Great Hall of the People was finished in only 10 months, a great wonder in the architectural history of China and of the world as well.

The National Museum of China 国家博物馆 is on the eastern side of the Tian'anmen Square. It was formally founded on February 28, 2003 on the basis of the former Museum of the Chinese Revolution and Museum of Chinese History. It is a comprehensive museum with history and culture as the mainstay, displaying the long culture and history of the Chinese nation in a systematic way.

① Tian' anmen Square
② A bird' s-eye view of Tian'anmen Square and the Forbidden City
③ The Monument to the People's Heroes
④ A group of sculptures in front of Chairman Mao's Memorial Hall
⑤ Chairman Mao's Memorial Hall
⑥ Great Hall of the People
⑦ National Museum of China

Shanghai Pudong New Area
– a New Modern City Zone

上海浦东新区——中国现代化的新城区

On the eastern bank of the Huangpu River in Shanghai, the Pudong New Area has a total area of 523 square kilometers and a population of 1.81 million. On April 18, 1990, the Chinese government made an important decision on developing and opening-up Pudong in Shanghai, which was called the largest development project in the world by foreigners. According to the strategic plan of the Party Central Committee, the Shanghai Municipal Government worked out the development policy of "developing Pudong, vitalizing Shanghai, serving the whole country and heading for the world market." After the painstaking efforts in the past 16 years, world-renowned achievements have been made in the development and opening-up of Pudong; the export-oriented, multi-function and modernized framework of a new city zone has taken shape; and Pudong has become a "window of China's reform and opening up," and an "epitome of the Shanghai modernization drive," creating a wonder of the construction of a modernized city in China.

The Oriental Pearl TV Tower 东方明珠广播电视塔，which is situated in Lujiazui in the Pudong New Area, is 468 meters high, the third tallest in the world. The construction of the tower began in July 1991, and was completed in 1994. It can receive 6,000 visitors a day.

Jinmao Tower 金茂大厦 is located in the Pudong New Area. It was built in 1998, 420.5 meters high, the tallest in the Chinese mainland. It has a floorage of 290,000 square meters. The main building has 88 stories (plus four stories at the top for mechanical and electrical equipment and three stories underground). It is a comprehensive building integrating offices, hotels and sightseeing. From the first to the 50th stories are offices, which can hold a total of 10,000 staff members; from the 51st and the 52nd stories are for the mechanical and electrical equipment; from the 53rd to the 87th stories are the hotel; and the 88th story is the Observation Hall, 340.1 meters high and with an area of 1,520 square meters. It is the highest and largest observation hall in China, at which visitors can have a panoramic view of Shanghai.

① Shanghai Pudong New Area
② Jinmao Tower

Ancient City of Jiaohe (Western Han to Yuan: 206 B.C.- A.D.1368) – a Wonder Preserved by Nature

交河故城(西汉－元代：前 206—1368)──被大自然保存下来的奇迹

Located in Yarhu Township, about 10 kilometers west of Turpan City in the Xinjiang Uygur Autonomous Region, the ancient city of Jiaohe was built at a place where two rivers meet, hence the name of the city Jiaohe (meaning a place where two rivers meet). As it is strategically situated and occupies a commanding position, the local people call it "Yarhetu," meaning "Cliff City." First constructed in the Western Han Dynasty (206-25 B.C.), Jiaohe was a political center of Turpan Area. In the Tang Dynasty (618-907), Jiaohe City was where Anxi Garrison, the highest military headquarters of the Western Regions, was stationed. After the end of the Yuan Dynasty (1206-1368) when Jiaohe was merged into Turpan, the ancient city was gradually abandoned.

The ruins in the ancient city were the architectural structures built after the Tang Dynasty. The city is 300 meters wide from east to west, and about 1,650 meters from south to north. In the shape of a large willow leave, with two pointed ends, the whole city has only one gate — South Gate, and does not have city walls, a phenomenon which is different from other ancient cities. The base of the city is 30 meters higher than the ground, making the city like an isolated island in a vast sea. The cliffs are sharp. We can imagine that in ancient times when people fought with arrows, swords and halberds, no enemies dared to approach this ancient city with such a natural barrier.

The ruins in the ancient city of Jiaohe mainly consist of three parts: temples, civilian houses and official residences. In the center of the city stands a temple, with an area of 5,000 square meters. Legend has it that it is the largest temple in the city. The well-preserved temple, 88 meters long and 58 meters wide, is encircled by rectangle earth walls, and has pagodas and corridors. In the north of the ancient city stands a large Buddhist pagoda built with rammed earth, several dozen meters high. Originally, the large pagoda was surrounded by 25 lesser pagodas. Eroded by the wind and sands in the past many years, all the small pagodas are gone, leaving behind only their bases.

✳   ✳   ✳   ✳   ✳   ✳   ✳   ✳

Ancient City of Gaochang (Western Han to Ming Dynasty: 206 B.C.- A.D.1664) – an Old City Preserved by Nature

高昌故城(西汉－明代：前206－1644)──被大自然保存下来的古城

About 40 kilometers southeast of Turpan in Xinjiang in northwest China, it is the ruins of the capital of the Kingdom of Gaochang (442-640), which was abolished in the early Ming Dynasty (1368-1644), with a history of over 1,500 years. Gaochang, which used to be the commercial capital on the ancient Silk Road, occupied an important position in Chinese history. The present-day ancient city of Gaochang covers an area about two million square meters, and the whole city was built with rammed earth. Due to the dry weather in Turpan, the ancient city has been preserved by nature.

The Ancient City of Gaochang has preserved the broken walls of the outer wall. The square city, about five kilometers in circumference, formally consisted of three

parts: outer city, inner city and palace city, which are faintly visible now. With criss-crossed streets, the city includes the markets, palace, official residences, monasteries and temples, which are all built with rammed earth. Eroded by the wind and sand storms, the roofs of the buildings are all gone, leaving only some yellow earth walls or broken courtyards. Some walls rise straight from the ground, and reach over 10 meters high, looking like small hills on the Loess Plateau. Ascending a height, visitors may see the old streets, small houses or kitchens. On the south-western corner of the outer city, there is a large ruin of a temple, with an area of 10,000 square meters. The temple's gate, square, halls, pagodas and niches for statues of Buddha are well preserved, and the doors, windows and niches can been seen clearly. Legend has it that the walls on the four sides of the temple are covered with colorful paintings on the Buddhist stories. The Ancient City of Gaochang is a wonder on the Ancient Silk Road between China and the countries in Central Asia in ancient times.

Ancient City of Suzhou (Song: 960-1279)
– the "Oriental Venice"

The Ancient City of Suzhou is located in Suzhou City, Jiangsu Province in east China. A famous historical and cultural city of China, Suzhou has a recorded history of over 4,000 years. Now the Ancient City of Suzhou still preserves the double-chessboard layout of the Song Dynasty, featuring "water and roads going side by side, and rivers bordering on streets." Suzhou has crisscrossed rivers, and the famous Grand Canal passes by the city. The rivers in the Ancient City of Suzhou total 35 kilometers long, with over 170 bridges, hence the name of the "Oriental Venice." Each of the eight city gates of Suzhou can be reached by both land and water. As the city is linked with the countryside by roads and rivers, Suzhou has convenient transport facilities. Tourists can go to the beautiful city by automobile or boat.

Suzhou is a noted garden city in China. An old saying goes: "South China has the most beautiful gardens in the country; and Suzhou has the most beautiful gardens in South China." In the Ming (1368-1644) and Qing (1644-1911) dynasties, private gardens in Suzhou numbered over 200. Taking a walk in the ancient city, tourists can see the beautiful scenery of a land of water everywhere, with plaster walls, black tiles, small bridges, running waters and waterside houses. Suzhou is a famous tourist destination all the people are eager to go.

Old Town of Lijiang (Southern Song: 1127-1279) – a Mysterious Town of the Naxi People

丽江古城（南宋：1127–1279）——纳西族的神秘古城

Located in the old area of Lijiang City, Yunnan Province in southwest China, the Old Town is a place where the Naxi ethnic minority people live in compact communities. First constructed in the last year of the Southern Song Dynasty, the Old Town of Lijiang covers an area of 1.5 square meters, and is skirted by hills and waters on the four sides. It is in the shape of a large inkslab, hence the name "Large Inkslab City." Almost all the ancient cities in China have city walls, but the Old Town of Lijiang is an exception. Legend has it that Lijiang was under the reign of the hereditary Mu family for a long time. If the Chinese character Mu ("木" that represents the governor of Lijiang) is put into a frame ("口" represents the city wall), there will be the character "困" which means "siege" or

"predicament." This would mean that the governing Mu family and their descendants would always be in a difficult position. Because of

this symbolism, Old Town Lijiang was never given a city wall. The square streets in the Old Town are all paved by slabstones, and the streets are lined by earth-and-wood houses covered with tiles, plus over 350 stone and wooden bridges. Limpid spring water flows into all the streets and lanes in the Old Town, and weeping willows grow lushly by the streets and waters, presenting a fascinating picture.

The Naxi people have believed in their primitive religion, Dongba Sect, for nearly 1,000 years. Influenced by Bonism, Buddhism and Taoism, Dongba Sect maintains its own ethnic group's Dongba written language, ceremonies, classics, music, dances and paintings. In particular, the melodious Naxi ancient music and the mysterious Dongba pictorgraphy have attracted the attention of numerous Chinese and foreign tourists. The Old Town of Lijiang has been included in the World Heritage List by the UNESCO.

Ancient City of Pingyao (Ming: 1368-1644)
– the "Turtle City"

平遥古城(明代:1368—1644)——被称为"龟城"

Situated in the seat of Pingyao County in Shanxi Province in central China, the ancient city was built in the third year of the Hongwu reign period (1370) of the Ming Dynasty. The square city wall built with bricks is 6.4 kilometers in circumference, 12 meters high and five meters wide on average. The watchtowers were built on the outer wall at 50-meter intervals, and there is a corner tower on each of the four corners. On the city wall, there are 3,000 battlements and 72 watchtowers, symbolizing that Confucius had 3,000 disciples, of whom 72 were outstanding. Certainly, it is a coincidence. The city wall was built in the shape of a turtle with six gates, hence the name "Turtle City." A bird's-eye view will find that the city is surrounded by a moat, and the city wall has six gates: One on the south, one on the north, two on the east and two on the west. The gates on the south and north walls symbolize the head and tail of the turtle, and the gates on the east and west walls stand for the feet. In ancient China, the turtle is an auspicious animal, symbolizing longevity and as solid as a rock.

All the streets, houses and shops in the ancient city of Pingyao remain intact. The government residences, altars, temples and other large architectural structures in the old city are laid out according to the ranking system of traditional rites, which is a rare

living example for the modern people to study the organizational system of a county and the military defensive system in ancient China. The Ancient City of Pingyao has been included in the World Heritage List by the UNESCO.

The Ancient City Wall of Nanjing (Ming: 1368-1644)
– the Longest City Wall in the World

南京古城墙(明代：1368－1644)——世界上最长的城墙

Nanjing, the capital of Jiangsu Province in east China, was an ancient capital of China. The construction of the capital city began in 1366 and was completed in 1393, lasting a total of 28 years. According to the information issued by the Nanjing Cultural Relics Bureau on February 16, 2006, the city wall of Nanjing built in the Ming Dynasty is 35.267 kilometers long, of which 22.425 kilometers have been basically well preserved. The city wall is 26 meters high; the narrowest spot is 2.6 meters; and the widest spot is 19.75 meters. The existing moat totals 31.159 kilometers long, 334 meters at the widest and nine

meters at the narrowest. With granites as the foundation, the city wall of Nanjing, built with large-sized bricks, contains 2,000 fortresses and 13,616 crenels. Lying at the foot of a mountain and by a river, the city wall is the largest one in the world, and a wonder of China's ancient capital cities.

Zhonghua Gate 中华门 is the south gate of the walled capital city of Nanjing in the early Ming Dynasty. In the shape of a rectangle, it is 24.5 meters high, 128 meters from south to north and 90 meters from east to west. With an area of 11,700 square meters, Zhonghua Gate is the largest and most magnificent of the 13 gates on the city wall of Nanjing built in the Ming Dynasty. The entire structure was built with large stone slabs and massive bricks mortared together with special cement made from lime and sticky rice juice. As a huge defensive military castle, Zhonghua Gate has three circular cities, which are linked by four arched doors. In ancient times, each gate had a large sluice gate that could be moved up and down, and two wooden doors. Twenty-seven tunnels were

built in the castle to store large quantities of food and weapons and to hold approximately 3,000 soldiers. If the enemies launched an attack on the city, the soldiers could lure them into the city, then closed all the city gates to separate the enemies into three parts and eliminate them one by one. It is so-called "catching a turtle in a jar" as described in the military books. With a complicated structure and a strong defensive force, the large Zhonghua Gate is an architectural wonder of the cities in China.

✳   ✳   ✳   ✳   ✳   ✳   ✳   ✳

The Ancient City Wall of Xi'an (Ming: 1368-1644) – the Most Complete City Wall in the World

西安古城墙（明代：1368—1644）——世界上最完整的城墙

Located in Xi'an City, Shaanxi Province   in northwest China, the city wall of Xi'an was first constructed on the basis of the capital city of Chang'an of the Tang Dyansty (618-907). It is one of the most famous ancient city wall

built in the late period of the feudal society in Chinese history, as well as the most complete and most magnificent castle-style architectural structure. The plane of the city wall is a rectangle, 12 meters high, 12 to 24 meters at the top and 15 to 18 meters at the bottom and 11.9 kilometers in circumference. The wall is built with black bricks. A total of 5,894 battlements stand on the wall. On the four corners of the city wall, there are turrets. Each side has a main city gate, and each gate-tower consists of three towers (Front Tower, Arrow Tower and Watchtower), the Circular City and a moat, forming a tight city defensive project. The city wall of Xi'an is an architectural wonder of the ancient capitals in China.

Chinese Temples

中国坛庙概述

Since ancient times, the Chinese people have had the fine tradition of offering sacrifices to ancestors. The emperors of the past dynasties called themselves the sons of Heaven, so that they needed to offer sacrifices to their ancestors, as well as to Heaven, earth, mountains and waters. Accordingly, various kinds of temples were built, such as Temple of Heaven, Temple of Earth, Temple of the Sun, Temple of Mountain God and Temple of Water God. On the lunar New Year's Day or other festivals, ordinary Chinese people hang the memorial tablets or portraits of their ancestors and hold the commemorative ceremony at home. The rich and large families have their own family temples or shrines to show their commemoration of their ancestors. If a place has a number of families of the same surname, the people of the same surname would have a public shrine built after consultation. Such clan shrines were often built with high-quality materials and decorated beautifully, and become the unique architectural structures of ancient China.

Temple and Cemetery of Confucius and the Kong Family Mansion in Qufu (479 B.C.-Present)
– the Hometown of Sage Confucius

曲阜三孔(孔府、孔庙、孔林)(前 479 至今)——中国圣人孔子的故乡

　　The Temple of Confucius, the Cemetery of Confucius and the Kong Family Mansion are located in the old city of Qufu City, Shandong Province in east China. Qufu is the hometown of Confucius. The name of Confucius (551-479 B.C.) is Qiu and he styled himself Zongni. Confucius was a famous thinker, statesman, educationist, and the founder of Confucianism at the end of the Spring and Autumn period (770-476 B.C.). Through giving lectures and revising *The Book of Odes* and *The Spring and Autumn Annals*, Confucius founded the Confucian School, which exerted profound influence on the feudal culture with a history of several thousand years. Hence, the rulers and feudal scholars of the past dynasties, who held the esteem of Confucius, had the Temple of Confucius, Cemetery of Confucius and Kong Family Mansion built in his hometown, which have been well known in the world and have

been included in the World Heritage List by the UNESCO.

The Temple of Confucius 孔庙 is located in the city proper of Qufu. It is where the people worship Confucius. According to historical records, Lord Ai of the state of Lu turned the three old houses of Confucius into the "Temple of Confucius" in the second year after Confucius's death. After the Western Han Dynasty (206 B.C.- A.D.25), the emperors of the successive dynasties kept giving Confucius posthumous titles and honors. As a result, the temple was continuously renovated and expanded until it became a magnificent architectural complex. With an area of over 218,000 square meters, the Temple of Confucius is over one kilometer long from south to north, and has a total of 466 halls, pavilions and side rooms. Surrounded by red walls, the Temple of Confucius includes nine courtyards; the roofs of the halls are covered

with yellow glazed tiles; and there are turrets on the four corners. The layout of the temple is similar to the imperial palace, and its size and scale are only next to the Forbidden City in Beijing. Dacheng Hall is the main building in the temple, where the memorial ceremony for Confucius is held. A horizontal inscribed board is hung at the center of the hall, with four Chinese characters reading: "Ultimate Sage, Foremost Teacher," and a statue of Confucius is enshrined in the hall. Rebuilt in the 13th year of the Hongzhi reign period (1500) of the Ming Dynasty, Dacheng Hall now is 32 meters high, 54 meters from south to west and 34 meters deep. The hall has double eaves, and the roof is in *xieshan* style (a traditional style of Chinese palace architecture, fully hipped on both sides, and half-hipped at the ends, so that an upper gable is left exposed), covered by glittering yellow tiles. Dacheng Hall has 32 red pillars made of

Marvels of China

3

nanmu (the fine-grained fragrant hardwood), each with a diameter of one meter; and the ceiling is inlaid with 486 pieces colorful boards, looking just like the Hall of Golden Chimes in the former Imperial Palace in Beijing. In particular, Dacheng Hall has 10 huge stone pillars, which are entwined with dragons amidst clouds, rockeries and waves carved in high bas-relief. They are the precious stone carvings of ancient China, showing high craftsmanship. Legend has it that when the emperor came here to pay homage to Confucius, the pillars would be covered with red cloths, because they are even larger and more magnificent than the dragon pillars in the imperial palace. With carved beams and painted pillars, the resplendent Temple of Confucius is the largest and oldest temple built for a scholar in Chinese history, hence it is a wonder in the Chinese architectural history, and even an architectural wonder in the world.

The Kong Family Mansion 孔府 is situated in the city proper of Qufu, and borders the Temple of Confucius. Before the founding of New China in 1949, it was the official mansion of Duke Yansheng and the private residence of the eldest son and eldest grandson of the descendants of Confucius.

First constructed in the first year of the Baoyuan reign period (1038) of the Northern Song Dynasty, it was rebuilt in the 10th year of the Hongwu reign period (1377) of the Ming Dynasty, and was renovated time and again later. The mansion covers an area of 16 hectares, and has nine courtyards and 463 halls, towers and studios and three routes. The eastern route is the Kong family's temple; the western route was the place where Duke Yansheng read books and poems, and learnt etiquettes; and the houses along the middle route are offices, including three main rooms and nine halls, with residences at the rear, which are linked with a garden. Tightly guarded and luxuriously decorated, the Kong Family Mansion is a typical feudal aristocratic manor integrating an official mansion and a private residence. With a large number of precious cultural relics, it is a museum of the Kong family. The Kong Family Mansion is the largest and oldest private residence in China as well as in the world.

The Cemetery of Confucius 孔林 is about one kilometer north of Qufu City. It is a cemetery specially for Confucius and his descendants, and the largest, oldest and best-preserved ancient family cemetery in the

4

Chinese Temples

⑤

the first three generations have the well-preserved gravestones, shrines, sacred paths and stone statues, the locations of the tombs of the descendants from the fourth to the seventh generations of the Kong family can be roughly known according to the drawing of the Cemetery of Confucius; and no traces can be discovered for the tombs of the descendants of the seventh to the 41st generations of the Kong family. The tombs built in the Yuan, Ming and Qing dynasties (1206-1911) have been basically well preserved. Surrounded by red walls, the tomb of Confucius is in an independent graveyard in the cemetery. The tomb of Confucius is 8.2 meters high and 88 meters in circumference. In front of the tomb stands a stone tablet set up in the eighth year of the Zhengtong reign period (1440) of the Ming Dynasty, with an inscription: "Tomb of Great Perfection, Ultimate Sate and Culture-Propagating King." On the left side of the tomb is the tomb of Kong Li, son of Confucius, and in the front of the tomb of Confucius is the tomb of Kong Ji, grandson of Confucius. The layout of the three tombs in the shape of " 品 " is known as "Confucius bringing his son along and holding his grandson in the arms." To the western side of the tomb of Confucius, there is a small hut, known as the "Hut Where Zi Gong Guarded the Tomb." According to historical records, after Confucius had been buried, his disciples were in mourning for three years for him, but only Zi Gong built a hut beside the tomb and refused to leave before he had guarded the tomb for six years, expressing his deep love for his teacher. On the eastern side of the tomb of Confucius are three pavilions,

world. At the beginning, the cemetery only occupied an area of one hectare. Over the last 2,400 years, all the descendants of Confucius and the members of the Kong clan were buried here. The emperors of the past dynasties constantly bestowed graveyards to the Kong family, making the cemetery become larger and larger. In the Qing Dynasty (1644-1911), the Cemetery of Confucius occupied an area of two million square meters, and over seven kilometers in circumference. The cemetery, a rarely seen artificial garden, grows about 100,000 tall trees, of which over 20,000 are ancient trees. Historical records reveal that the disciples of Confucius brought about rare species of trees from their hometowns throughout the country and grew them in the cemetery; hence the cemetery has a wide variety of species of trees. The cemetery also contains a great number of tombs, stone tablets and steles, hence the name the "Forest of Steles." About 77 generations of the descendants of the Kong family after Confucius are buried in the Kong family graveyard. With the passage of time, except for the tombs of called the "pavilions where the emperors stayed temporarily." Legend has it that when Emperor Zhenzhong of the Song Dynasty, and emperors Kangxi and Qianlong of the Qing Dynasty came here to pay homage to Confucius, they once stayed in the pavilions. The Cemetery of Confucius is a wonder of the Chinese family tombs.

① Dacheng Hall of the Temple of Confucius
② Temple of Confucius
③ Front Hall of the Kong Family Mansion
④ Cemetery of Confucius
⑤ Temple of Confucius

*　　　*　　　*　　　*　　　*　　　*　　　*

Temple of Heaven (Ming and Qing: 1368-1911) – the Place for the Emperors to Worship Heaven

天坛(明清：1368—1911)——皇帝祭天的地方

Situated on the southern corner of Beijing, the Temple of Heaven was first constructed in the 18th year of the Yongle reign period (1420) of the Ming Dynasty, with an area of 2.73 million square meters, over twice larger than the former Imperial Palace. The Temple of Heaven ranks first of the six major temples in Beijing — Temple of Heaven, Temple of Earth, Temple of the Sun, Temple of the Moon, Temple of the Gods of Agriculture and Temple of Imperial Divine. As the largest temple architectural complex in China, the Temple of Heaven was where the emperors of the Ming and Qing dynasties worshipped Heaven and prayed for a good harvest.

In the Temple of Heaven, there are two altars: Inner Altar and Outer Altar, which are enclosed by the inner and outer walls. The wall at the northern end is circular, representing Heaven, and the wall at the southern end is square, representing earth. This layout conforms to a traditional saying in ancient China: The heaven is a sphere, and the earth is square. The north wall is higher than the south wall, indicating the cultural connotations that the heaven is high, and the earth is low. The main architectural structures in the Temple of Heaven from south to north include the Circular Mound Altar, Imperial Vault of Heaven, Hall of Prayer for Good Harvests and Hall of Imperial Heaven. The Palace of Abstinence is within the west wall of the Inner Altar, and the Office of Divine Music is within the west wall of the Outer Altar. To link heaven with the earth, the Cinnabar Stairway Bridge, 360 meters long, was built along the south-north central axis.

The Circular Mound Altar (Yuanqiutan) 圜丘坛 is located in the south of the Temple of Heaven, where the emperor offered sacrifices to heaven at the time of the winter solstice every year; hence it is also called the Altar for Offering Sacrifices to Heaven, or the Altar for Worshipping Heaven. This three-tiered white stone terrace is enclosed by two walls, the inner one round and the outer one square. The altar was constructed with nine or multiples of nine stone slabs. For instance, the upper balustrades were built with 72 slabs; the middle guardrail, 108; and the lower guardrail, 180, totaling 360 slabs, a number equivalent to the 360 degrees of the great circle of the celestial sphere. In ancient times, since nine was considered the most powerful number, nine was used to symbolize the supreme "heaven." If you stand in the center of the top terrace, known the Supreme Ultimate Stone or the Heavenly Heart Stone, and speak with a normal volume, your voice will sound louder and more resonant to yourself than to others standing around, making you feel mysterious.

The Imperial Vault of Heaven (Huangqiongyu) 皇穹宇 is to the north of the Circular Mound Altar, where the tablet of the supreme sovereign god of heaven is placed. The main hall is round, symbolizing heaven, which enshrines the tablet of the "Supreme Ruler of Heaven." In ancient China, after the sacrificial ceremony, the emperor would send the tablet back to the Imperial

❶

❷

Vault of Heaven. On either the eastern or western side of the main hall, there are five small side rooms for holding the tablets of other heavenly gods, such as the sun, moon, star, rain, wind, thunder and lightning gods. Around the Imperial Vault of Heaven and the eastern and western side rooms is the famous Echo Wall, built according to the principle that a sound wave bounces off a curved wall many times in succession. A whisper at one point of the wall can be heard clearly at an opposite point. In front of the main hall are the Three Echo Stones. A handclap on the third stone produces a triple echo.

The Red Stairway Bridge (Danbiqiao) 丹陛桥 is also known as the Sacred Way or the Way to Heaven. It is a 360-meter-long stone passage that leads from the Imperial Vault of Heaven to the Hall of Prayer for Good Harvests. The bridge, or the causeway, represents the distance between heaven and the earth. You can see five parallel paths on the bridge. The central protruding path, called the "Sacred Path," was for the god of heaven; the left path was reserved for the emperor; the right path was used by princes and ministers; and the two outside paths were for ordinary officials. The architectural structures along the axial line from south to north are one higher than another, symbolizing that "Heaven is high and the earth is low." On both sides of the passage lushly grow pine and cypress trees. Strolling along the passage, visitors will find the sky is high and the land is vast, and feel as if they were in a fairyland.

The Hall of Prayer for Good Harvests (Qiniandian) 祈年殿 is in the north of the Temple of Heaven, and is a circular wooden structure, 38 meters high and 32.71 meters in diameter. It has a triple conical roof set with deep blue glazed tiles and topped with a large

gold-plating knob. The building stands on a three-tiered circular terrace surrounded by white marble balustrades, looking grand and magnificent. On the first *xin* day (a special day in the first 10 days of the first lunar month every year, which was designated on the third *xin* day in the last 10 days of the 12th lunar month of the previous year through the practice of divination) every year, the emperor held a solemn ceremony here to pray for a good harvest and favorable weather. The four central pillars symbolize the four seasons of the year. Around them is an inner circle of 12 pillars, symbolizing the 12 months of the lunar calendar, and beyond is an outer circle of another 12, symbolizing the 12 two-hour periods into which the cycle of day and night was traditionally divided.

The Palace of Abstinence (Zhaigong) 斋宫 is to the south of the West Heavenly Gate of the Temple of Heaven, which is a square city, with an area of 40,000 square meters. It was the place where the emperor resided and took a rest before a memorial ceremony. The hall was built according to an old rite: "Food must be changed for fasting; and a new dwelling must be taken for abstinence." Before the ceremony for offering sacrifices to Heaven, the emperor held a three-day fast at the Hall of Abstinence. To show the respect for the "Supreme Ruler of Heaven," the Palace of Abstinence was built beside the Temple of Heaven, and the roofs are covered with green glazed tiles (The green roof was only for the residences of officials), rather than the yellow glazed tiles, which were for the roofs of the imperial palace, conveying the meaning that even the emperor was only an official in front of the ruler of Heaven. The main hall in the Palace of Abstinence is beamless, with the implied meaning that the emperor respected Heaven with absolute sincerity like the beamless hall.

The design, layout and colors of the Temple of Heaven symbolize "Heaven," full of illusions and superstitions. The Temple of Heaven

is a product of the combination of the feudal political power and religious authority. Its unique and beautiful architectural style is the only one of its kind in the world, and a great wonder in the world architectural history created by the Chinese nation. The Temple of Heaven has been included in the World Heritage List by the UNESCO.

① Imperial Vault of Heaven
② Circular Mound Altar
③ Hall of Prayer for Good Harvests
④ Red Stairway Bridge
⑤ Beamless Hall in the Palace of Abstinence

* * * * * * * *

Chen Clan Shrine (Qing: 1644-1911) – an Ordinary Clan Temple in China

陈家祠(清代：1644—1911)——中国老百姓的家庙

Located in Guangzhou, Guangdong Province in southeast China, the Chen Clan Shrine is also known as the Chen Clan Academy, which is an architectural complex showing the most characteristics of carving art in the existing shrines in China.

Constructed from the 16th to the 20th year (1890-1894) of the Guangxu reign period in the Qing Dynasty, it is a clan shrine built with the funds raised by the people with the surname of Chen from the 72 counties in Guangdong Province to worship their ancestors. With an area of over 13,000 square meters, and a floorage of 6,400 square meters, the shrine consists of three rows of large halls, more than 80 meters long; four long corridors in the middle and on the right and left sides; and six courtyards. The large halls on the first row used to be the sitting room and a private school (In old China, it was very common that a private school was attached to the clan shrine); the halls on the second row were meeting halls; and the halls on the third row held the tablets of the ancestors. The tablets of those with high fame and positions are placed in the middle; and the tablets of those with low fame and positions on both sides, with a strict hierarchy.

The most characteristic of the Chen Clan Shrine is the beautiful and exquisite carved decorations, showing high craftsmanship. All the halls, courtyards, corridors, halls, doors, windows, balustrades, and ridges in the shrine are decorated with stone, wood and brick carvings, pottery wares, clay sculptures and iron castings. They include exquisite ornaments in the shapes of melons, fruits, flowers, birds, cloud patterns and cast iron flowers on the stone balustrades, as well as clay sculptures, 27 meters long and two meters high, which are placed on the ridges of the roofs. The architectural decorative works of art involve various kinds of themes, such as historical stories and legends, and the patterns showing the landscapes, villages, pavilions and kiosks in the area south of the Five Ridges. Most of the sculptures and colorful paintings reflect the laboring people's wish for a bumper grain harvest and all thriving of the domestic animals, and display the fruits of south China, such as pineapples, litchis, parambolas and pawpaws. The Chen Clam Shrine that integrates all kinds of folk arts is a wonder among all the shrines of China.

In 1958, the Chen Clan Shrine became the Guangdong Folk Art Museum, combining this famous architecture with local characteristics with rich and colorful folk works of art in Guangdong. It always attracts lots of Chinese and foreign visitors.

Chinese Gardens

中国园林概述

In general, Chinese gardens can be classified into imperial gardens and private gardens. The imperial gardens first appeared in the early Western Zhou Dynasty (1046-771 B.C.), and were developed and grew in strength from the Spring and Autumn period (770-476 B.C.) to the Qin and Han dynasties (221 B.C.- A.D.220). The imperial gardens had the same functions as the imperial palace, aiming to show the great power of the emperor.

Chinese gardens focus on temperament and tastes. The design of a Chinese garden takes into account of the exchange of feelings between man and nature. In general, Chinese gardens consist of four main elements: artificial hills, waters, buildings and flowers & trees. The rocks, hills, lakes, pavilions, kiosks, cobblestone paths, flowers, grasses and greens can be arranged in a garden as one wishes, unlike the programmed gardens in the Western countries which look unnatural. The Chinese gardens display the gardening method — "though artificially built, they look natural," with a well-conceived layout, winding paths, hollowed lake stones, varied flowers and trees, and different landscapes. When strolling in a garden, visitors cannot see its end, but enjoy different landscapes and the beauty of nature through the zigzagging corridors, walls and windows with changeable patterns, pavilions and terraces in picturesque disorder.

Gardens in Suzhou (Ming and Qing: 1368-1911)
– the Most Beautiful Classical Gardens in China

苏州园林(明清:1368—1911)——中国最美的古典园林

Situated in Jiangsu Province in east China, Suzhou is a famous historical and cultural city in China, with a history of 2,500 years and numerous famed historical sites. Suzhou is a city of gardens, and the classical gardens in Suzhou are wonders among the Chinese gardens.

With a time-honored history, Suzhou City was formed in the Spring and Autumn period (770-476 B.C.), and became flourishing in the Tang and Song dynasties (618-1279). In the period of great prosperity of the Ming and Qing dynasties, Suzhou had over 200 gardens in various sizes, of which 69 have been well preserved. Most of the classical gardens in Suzhou are private gardens, small and exquisite. As befitting the Chinese style of garden culture, a limited space is ingeniously grouped into kaleidoscopic scenery to make people enjoy varied picturesque landscapes in a small garden without going outdoors. Suzhou gardens have developed a school of their own. The Humble Administrator's Garden, Lingering Garden and Fisherman's

1

2

Garden are the representatives of the classical gardens in Suzhou.

Humble Administrator's Garden
(Zhuozhengyuan)拙政园 is situated on the
northern corner of the ancient city of Suzhou,
and is the largest classical garden in Suzhou.
In the early Tang Dynasty (618-907), it was
the residence of a poet Lu Guimeng. During
the Zhengde reign period (1506-1521) of the
Ming Dynasty, Wang Xianchen, an imperial
censor who could not get along well with in-
fluential officials at the court, handed in his
resignation and returned home in Suzhou. He
bought a piece of land at his hometown, and
had the private garden built, where he lived
in seclusion. He named the garden
Zhuozhengyuan, meaning that a person who
was unable to serve as an official for the state
could only grow flowers and vegetables at
home, bragging about being aloof from petty
politics and material pursuits, and expressing
the feeling of a frustrated official in the feudal society. The garden as it stands today falls
into eastern, central and western parts. It
seems that a pagoda stood in the back of the
garden. As a matter of fact, the pagoda is one
kilometer from the garden. The architect de-
liberately "borrowed" it to match the scenery
in the garden. In the Chinese gardening art, it
is called the "method of using the scenery
outside a garden to harmonize with that
within."

Lingering Garden (Liuyuan)留园,
which is situated in Liuyuan Road in northwest Suzhou, is one of the famous gardens in
Suzhou. First constructed in the Jiajing reign
period (1522-1566) of the Ming Dynasty, it
was a private garden of Xu Shitai, a high-ranking official. With an area of 33,000 square
meters, the garden is divided into the central,
eastern and western parts. The central zone is
composed of a sparkling pond surrounded by
artificial hills, waterside pavilions, small
bridges and corridors. All the scenic spots in
the garden are linked by a 700-meter-long
winding corridor.

an official by the name of Song Zongyuan, who converted it into a garden, and called himself "Fisherman," hence the present name of the garden. With an area about 5,000 square meters, the garden is a typical complex of dwelling houses attached with a garden in old China. The garden can generally fall into the eastern, central and western parts. The West Garden, which used to be the place where the owner read books and cultivated his moral characters, has a tranquil environment and shows the typical architectural style of the Ming Dynasty (1368-1644). Its reproduction — the "Ming Garden" — was built at the Metropolitan Museum of Art, New York in May 1980, setting a precedent of exporting Chinese gardens. The gardens in Suzhou have been included in the World Heritage List by the UNESCO.

Fisherman's Garden (Wangshiyuan)网师园, situated in Shiquan Street in southeast Suzhou, was the former residence of a retired official Shi Zhengzhi of the Southern Song Dynasty (1127-1279), which was called "Fishermen's Hermitage." During the Qianlong reign period (1736-1795) of the Qing Dynasty, the place fell into the hands of

① Humble Administrator's Garden
② Humble Administrator's Garden
③ Lingering Garden
④ Fisherman's Garden

Ruins of the Yuanmingyuan (Qing Dynasty: 1644-1911)
– a Burnt-down Imperial Garden

圆明园遗址(清代:1644–1911)——被纵火烧残的遗址

Located in Haidian District, Beijing, the ruins of the Yuanmingyuan (Park of Perfection and Brightness) were originally a large imperial garden, with an area of about 3.5 million square meters and over 10 kilometers in circumference. The park was first constructed in the 48th year of the Kangxi reign period (1709) of the Qing Dynasty, and was undertaken large-scale expansion in the Yongzheng and Qianlong reign periods. It took six emperors of the Qing government more than 150 years to finish this imperial garden, integrating the ancient, modern, Chinese and foreign gardening arts and becoming a park of unprecedented size and grandeur in the world, known as the "Garden of Gardens." The park had over 140 buildings, terraces, halls, pavilions, kiosks and towers. After digging lakes, building artificial hills, growing exotic flowers and rare herbs, moving hills and reducing land, over 100 landscapes were created. The landscaping was based on the famous gardens of south China. In addition, the park also included a group of European-style buildings, which belonged to the European-style Palace, and contained a great number of ancient books, paintings, calligraphic works, cultural relics and treasures. Hence it was also known as the Chinese Warehouse of Culture and Art. During the Qing Dynasty, the emperor lived and handled state affairs in the Yuanmingyuan over six months every year. Actually, the Yuanmingyuan was the second imperial palace in Beijing.

In the 10th year of the Xianfeng reign period (1860) of the Qing Dynasty, the Anglo-French joint forces invaded Beijing. After

plundering all the treasures in the park at will, they set fire to the whole park, destroying the world-renowned park in one day and leaving only some broken stone carvings of the European-style buildings in the Garden of Eternal Spring. The European-style buildings modeled on the Swiss and French palaces originally covered an area of about 67,000 square meters. The construction of the European-style Palace began in the 12th year of the Qianlong reign period (1747) of the Qing Dynasty, and completed in the 24th year of the Qianlong reign period (1759). All the buildings were built with white stones, and the carved Western patterns can also be seen on the broken stone pillars, showing the baroque style of the European Renaissance period. But all the roofs of the European-style buildings were covered with glazed tiles, and the indoor decoration showed traditional Chinese art. The European-style buildings displayed the harmonious combination of the Chinese and Western architectural styles, forming a unique style in the Chinese architectural history.

Now the ruins of the Yuanmingyuan have become an important center for patriotic education in China.

Summer Palace (Qing: 1644-1911) – the Most Beautiful Imperial Garden in China

颐和园(清代：1644—1911)——中国景物最丰富的皇家园林

Situated in Haidian District in Beijing, the Summer Palace was a temporary dwelling place of the emperors of the Qing Dynasty. It is a famous classical garden in north China, as well as the best-preserved imperial garden with the richest landscapes, and the most ar-

1

chitectural structures in the world. First constructed in the 15th year of the Qianlong reign period (1750) of the Qing Dynasty, it was originally named the Garden of Clear Ripples, which was destroyed by the Anglo-French joint forces in 1860. In the 14th year of the Guangxu reign period (1888), Empress Dowager Cixi spent five million tales of silver had it rebuilt under the pretext of building a naval training site, renamed it the Summer Palace, and made it her summer resort and pleasure garden. The palace mainly consists of Longevity Hill and Kunming Lake, occupies an area of 2.9 million meters and possesses more

than 3,000 various types of architectural structures. The Summer Palace entails a combination of all types of Chinese garden art and enjoys a very high position in the history of the Chinese garden art. It is mainly composed of three parts for holding court, residing and sightseeing, respectively. The main tourist attractions include a great number of beautiful architectural structures, such as the Pavilion of Buddhist Incense, the Palace Theater in the Garden of Harmonious Virtue, the Hall of Dispelling Clouds, the Long Corridor, the Marble Boat, the Pavilion of Precious Clouds (Baoyunge), the Bronze Ox, the 17-Arch Bridge and the Jade-Belt Bridge, which are all treasures of the world architectural art. Now all the halls in the Summer Palace are arranged according to their original state, hence the name the "Museum Park."

The Pavilion of Buddhist Incense (Foxiangge)佛香阁 stands at the top of Longevity Hill. The three-story pavilion has eight sides and four eaves, and sits on a 20-meter

③

stone terrace, 41 meters high. The magnificent pavilion is the central structure and the symbol of the Summer Palace.

The Theater 大戏楼 was the place for Empress Dowager Cixi to watch operas. The

④

three-storeyed theatre has a double roof with upturned eaves, 21 meters high, and the lowest stage is 17 meters wide. It was the largest theater in the Qing Dynasty. Each stage and its ceiling have trap-doors for actors playing gods or ghosts to enter and exist. At the basement of the stage, there are ponds and wells for creating water setting.

The Long Corridor 长廊 lies at the southern foot of Longevity Hill and along the northern bank of Kunming Lake. It measures 728 meters long and is divided by crossbeams into 273 sections. Located along the corridor are four octagonal pavilions, which symbolize spring, summer, autumn, and winter. The beams and ceiling of the corridor have over 8,000 paintings of flowers, birds, fish, insects, and famous Chinese buildings and landscapes, hence another name the Art Gallery. However, the most interesting are paintings of episodes from Chinese classical literature, folk tales as well as historical and legendary figures, each painting telling an interesting story.

The Clear and Calm Boat (Qingyanfang) 清晏舫 was originally known

■ Chinese Gardens

as the Marble Boat. It lies at the western foot of Longevity Hill and by Kunming Lake. It was first constructed in the 20th year of the Qianlong reign period (1755) of the Qing Dynasty. There used to be a Chinese-style wooden superstructure on the top part of the boat, but it was destroyed by the Anglo-French joint forces in 1860. In the 19th year of the Guangxu reign period (1893), a new super-structure modeled on those of foreign plea-sure boats was rebuilt.

The boat was named ac-cording to an old saying — "The rivers are clear, and the seas are calm," implying that the coun-try is at peace. The two-deck boat is 36 meters long. Although made of wood, the superstruc-ture is painted white, looking like a marble boat, and the top of the boat is decorated with carved bricks, looking exquisite and gorgeous.

The Pavilion of Precious Clouds (Baoyunge) 宝云阁 is commonly known as the Bronze Pavilion. It is on the western side of the Pavilion of the Buddhist Incense, 7.55 meters high and weighing 207 tons. The en-tire structure including its roof and columns is cast in bronze. Exquisite and dignified, the Bronze Pavilion is rare in the world.

The Bronze Ox 铜牛 is located near the 17-Arch Bridge in the Summer Palace. The

beautifully shaped Bronze Ox was cast in the 20th year of the Qianlong reign period (1755) of the Qing Dynasty. It was said that in ancient times, whenever Yu the Great put flood under control, he would put an iron ox in the riverbed, as ox was a symbol of flood control. After Kunming Lake was dredged, Emperor Qianlong cast a bronze ox and put it on the eastern shore of the lake according to the ancient custom, and cast the "Golden Ox Inscription" on the back of the ox to record the event.

Jade-Belt Bridge 玉带桥 is on the western causeway of Kunming Lake in the Summer Palace. There are a total of six bridges on the lake, of which the Jade-Belt Bridge is the most beautiful. Built with white marble stones,

the bridge carved with flying cranes in the clouds has a high and thin arch, showing a smooth line. In the shape of a jade belt, the semicircle bridge opening forms a transparent full moon together with its reflection on the water. The Summer Palace has been included in the World Heritage List by the UNESCO.

---

① Kunming Lake and Longevity Hill
② Pavilion of Buddhist Incense
③ The Theater
④ Long Corridor
⑤ The Bronze Ox
⑥ Pavilion of Precious Clouds
⑦ The Clear and Calm Boat
⑧ Jade-Belt Bridge

Summer Mountain Resort (Qing: 1644-1911) – the Largest Imperial Palace in China

避暑山庄(清代：1644—1911)——中国现存最大的皇家园林

Situated in Chengde City, Hebei Province in north China, the Summer Mountain Resort is over 200 kilometers south of Beijing. It was the place where the emperors of the Qing Dynasty spent summers and handled state af-

fairs in hot summers. The mountain resort was first built in the 42nd year of the Kangxi reign period (1703) of the Qing Dynasty, and after 89 years of painstaking efforts, it was completed in the 57th year of the Qianlong reign

2

period (1792). With an area of about 5.64 million square meters, the summer resort is twice the size of the Summer Palace in Beijing, and is the largest classical imperial garden in China. The resort itself falls into two parts: Palace Area and Garden Area

The Palace Area 宫殿区, which consists of four groups of quadrangle-style architectural structures built with black bricks and gray tiles, was a place north of the Great Wall where the emperors of the Qing Dynasty resided and handled state affairs.

The Garden Area 苑景区 consists of three major zones: Lake Zone, Plain Zone and Hill Zone, which have dense forests, undulating hills, grasslands and lakes with ripples, with fascinating landscapes formed by real waters and hills. According to statistics, the Garden Area has over 120 groups of ancient architectural complexes, with a total floorage of more than 100,000 square meters. The architectural structures in the Summer Mountain Resort are not as resplendent and magnificent as the former Imperial Palace in Beijing as they are covered with gray tiles, but they show a unique style.

Eight Outer Temples 外八庙 To the east and north of the Mountain Resort, there are a number of Buddhist monasteries and temples, known as the Eight Outer Temples. If we liken the Mountain Resort to a bright moon, the eight temples in the surrounding areas are like the stars, implying that a myriad of stars surround the moon, and all rivers empty into the sea. The Qing rulers had a number of temples built in diversified architectural styles with the Mountain Resort as the center to symbolize the centripetal force of all the ethnic groups in China to the central government, as well as the strength and re-unification in the "heydays of the Kangxi and Qianlong reign periods." Hence the Eight Outer Temples are not only a museum of China's national artistic architecture, but also the symbol of the great unity of all the ethnic groups.

Hall of Frugality and Placidity (Danbao Jingcheng) 澹泊敬诚, with an area of 583 square meters, is the main hall of the Mountain Resort, also known as Nanmu Hall because it was built of the fine-grained fragrant hardwood called *nanmu,* which can dispel flies and mosquitoes in summer. The hall is built with black bricks and plain tiles, and the *namu* is not painted, looking solemn and graceful, full of flavor of life. For 150 years from the Kangxi reign period to the Xianfeng reign period, the Hall of Frugality and Placidity served as the second policy center of the Qing government.

House of Mists and Rains 烟雨楼 is located on Green Lotus Islet north of Ruyi Islet in the Lake Area. During his inspection of south China, Emperor Qianlong of the Qing Dynasty was very fond of the House of Mists and Rains on South Lake in Jiaxing, Zhejiang Province, which was exquisite and beautiful, so he had a painting of the house drawn. The

construction of the house, a copy of the tower on South Lake, began in the 45th year of the Qianlong reign period (1780), and was completed in the same year. The building has a three-bay front and two stories; each story has five rooms; and it is surrounded by railings.

To the east of the house is Qingyang Study; and to the west, Duishan Studio. At the commanding point of Chenghu Lake, the house is the best place for tourists to have a panoramic view of the scenery around.

Knowledge Imparting Hall (Wenjinge) 文津阁 is located in the west of the Plain Area in the Mountain Resort. It is one of the four major libraries in the Qing Dynasty. The Knowledge Imparting Hall once held a collection of 3.63 million copies of books, which are a cultural heritage of great value. Looking from the outside, the Knowledge Imparting Hall has two stories, but it actually has three stories, including an underground story, which was built to prevent the sunshine from directly illuminating on the books.

Statue of the 1,000-Armed-and-1,000-Eyed Avalokitesvara 千手千眼观

世音菩萨像 sits in the Great Buddha Building in the Temple of Universal Peace, one of the Eight Outer Temples. It is the largest wooden statue of Avalokitesvara in China who has 1,000 arms and 1,000 eyes, 22.28 meters high. There are three eyes on the face of Bodhisattva, indicating that he knows well the past, the present and the future. A small statue of Buddha of Boundlessness, teacher of Avalokitesvara, 1.2 meters high, stands on the head of Bodhisattva to show respect to his teacher. Except for the two hands that put the palms together before him, Avalokitesvara has 40 arms, holding the religious ritual implements, such as the sun, moon, bell and pestle. There is an eye on each arm. Forty times 25 (the 25 forms of existence in Buddhism) is 1,000. Hence the name the 1,000-Armed-and-1,000-Eyed Avalokitesvara.

Xumifushou Temple 须弥福寿之庙 is in the north of the Mountain Resort and to the west of the Temple of Universal Peace. It was the temporary residence of the Sixth Bainqen Lama. In the Tibetan language, "Xumifushou" means "Tashilhunpo," in which "Tashi" means happiness and longevity, and "lhunpo," "Sumeru." In the 45th year of the Qianlong reign period (1780) of the Qing Dynasty, the Sixth Bainqen Lama took 13 months and traveled over 10,000 kilometers to Chengde to offer birthday congratulations to Emperor Qianlong. The emperor, who paid great attention to this event, studied the Tibetan language hard, and issued an order that a temporary palace residence be built according to the Tashilhunpo Monastery in Xigaze where the Bainqen Lama lived. It took a year to finish the construction of the temporary

6

❼

residence for the honored guest where Bainqen Lama resided and preached Tibetan Buddhism. With an area of 37,900 square meters, the Xumifushou Temple contains the tablet pavilion, the glass memorial archway, Red Terrace, Hall of Wonderful Height and Solemnity, Hall of Auspiciousness and Joy in the Law, and the glazed Longevity Pagoda.

Hall of Wonderful Height and Solemnity (Miaogaozhuangyandian) 妙高庄严殿 is the main building in the Xumifushou Temple, the three-story hall has a double-eave four-angle roof covered with gold-plated bronze tiles and topped with a dharma-bell knob in the center. On each of the four ridges, there are two gold-plated dragons (each weighing about one ton), which are vivid and lifelike, trying to soar up. The cast of the eight gold dragons cost over 15,000 tales of gold. The roof of the hall is glittering under the

sunshine.

The Mountain Resort, which integrates the quintessence of the Chinese gardening art, is a wonder of all the gardens in China and in the world. It has been included in the World Heritage List by the UNESCO.

---

① Xumifushou Temple
② Eight Outer Temples
③ The indoor scene of the Hall of Frugality and Placidits
④ Small Potala Palace
⑤ Knowledge Imparting Hall
⑥ Hall of Wonderful Height and Solemnity
⑦ Summer Mountain Resort

Splendid China (New China: 1949-Present) – a Replica Park of All Scenic Wonders in China

锦绣中华微缩景区（新中国：1949 至今）——中国奇观一目了然

Located in Shenzhen, Guangdong Province in southeast China, the Splendid China was constructed from 1987 to 1989. With an area of 300,000 square meters, it is the largest park with the most replicas of China's scenic spots and historical sites in the world. The scale models are mainly in a ratio of 1:15 and the exhibits are positioned to replicate their geographical locations. A great deal of attention was paid to detail so as to ensure the miniatures truly represent their originals. Here visitors can see the replicas of nearly 100 natural and cultural wonders in China, such as the undulating Great Wall, the grand former Imperial Palace in Beijing, the Potala Palace, the Giant Buddha of Leshan, the mysterious terra cotta warriors and horses excavated from the Mausoleum of Emperor Qin Shihuang (First Emperor of the Qin Dynasty), the Stone Forests, the grotesque peaks of Huangshan Mountain, the Three Gorges on the Yangtze River, the beautiful scenery along the Lijiang River, West Lake in Hangzhou, the gardens of Suzhou, the Mogao Grottoes in Dunhuang, Zhaozhou Bridge, the Wooden Pagoda in Yingxian County, the Mausoleum of Yellow Emperor, the Mausoleum of Genghis Khan, the Ming Tombs, Sun Yat-sen Mausoleum, the Temple of Confucius, the Temple of Heaven, and so on. Except the fascinating miniature tourist attractions, visitors can also appreciate the art of "ceramic figures," which present the "Wedding Ceremony of Emperor Guangxu" in the former Imperial Palace, the "Memorial Ceremony for Confucius" in Qufu, the "Nadam Fair" in Inner Mongolia, and the "Bazar" in Kashi, Xinjiang. According to the statistics, the Splendid China holds more than 56,000 vivid and lifelike ceramic figures, each having its own unique costumes and facial expression. Visitors need to spend only half a day to appreciate all the wonderful scenes and folk customs in China. Hence it is a wonder of modernized gardening.

Chinese Gardens

China Folk Culture Village (New China: 1949-Present) – a Replica Park of the Customs of China's 56 Ethnic Groups

中华民俗文化村（新中国：1949 至今）——中国 56 个民族一目了然

Located in Shenzhen, Guangdong Province in southeast China, the China Folk Culture Village neighbors the Splendid China (a park with miniature scenic wonders in China). Constructed from 1990 to 1991, it covers an area of 180,000 square meters. The China Folk Culture Village gathers the cultural quintessence of multi ethnic groups in China, and shows the picturesque scenery of undulating

hills, hanging waterfalls and winding streams. Over 20 villages were constructed at a ratio of 1:1, which are all vivid and lifelike, including the Han representative architecture, such as quadrangles in Beijing, cave dwellings in north Shaánxi Province, and ancient streets in Huizhou, which will make visitors gasp in admiration. The villages of ethnic minorities display their unique characteristics, such as

the stone village of the Buyi people, the square or rectangular houses made of solid wood of the Mosuo people, the "mushroom houses" of the Hanis, the yurts of the Kazaks, the bamboo buildings of the Dais, the streets on water of the Tujias, the yurts of the Mongols, the lamaseries of the Tibetans, and the mud-and-wood houses of the Yis, which will help tourists have a taste of the customs and lifestyles of all the ethnic groups in China. The civilian residences of the Bai, Tibetan, Naxi, Korean and Gaoshan ethnic groups show different architectural styles; and in the Miao, Dong, Yao, Wa, Li and Jingpo villages, young men and women warmly welcome Chinese and foreign guests. Here, tourists can also appreciate the wooden bridge of Yangzhou, the stone bridge of Zhejiang, the Rain-and-Wind Bridge of the Dong people, and the rattan bridge of the Dulong people, as well as the forest of coconut trees of Hainan, and the ancient banyan trees from Xishuangbanna. If you come at right time, you will be able to experience some unique festivals of the minorities, such as the Water-Splashing Festival of the Dais, the Torch Festival of the Yis, the Flower Fair of the Huis, the Knife Bar Festival of the Lisus, etc. At night, various kinds of ethnic theatrical performances are put on, making the visit to the China Folk Cultural Village to the climax. In the China Folk Culture Village, additional attractions are to taste local snacks, appreciate handicrafts of different ethnic groups, and feel the 56 ethnic groups are like 56 flowers, belonging to a large family of China with rich and profound cultural connotations. The Splendid China and the China Folk Culture Village reflect the splendid history, culture and endless glamour of the Chinese nation.

Window of the World (New China: 1949-Present)
– a Replica Park of World Marvels

世界之窗（新中国：1949至今）——世界奇观一目了然

Situated in Shenzhen, Guangdong in southeast China, it is adjacent to the Splendid China with miniature scenic wonders in the country and the China Folk Culture Village. Constructed in 1994, the Window of the World integrates the famous scenic spots, historical sites, natural scenery, civilian residences of different countries, foreign sculptures, folk customs and lifestyles, folk songs and dances in the world. Through the Window of the World, tourists can have a good understanding of the world's marvels.

The Window of World falls into nine zones according to the geological locations of the famous sites of different countries in the world and the sightseeing and activity contents, namely, World Square, Asia Zone, Europe Zone, Africa Zone, America Zone, Oceania Zone, Modern Scientific and Technological Recreational Zone, World Sculptures Zone and International Streets. The park contains a total of 118 world-renowned tourist attractions, including the Pyramids of Egypt, Angkor Wat of Cambodia, Grand Canal of the United States, Arch of Triumph of Paris, Saint Peter's Church in Vatican, Taj Mahal of India, Sydney Opera House of Australia, Leaning Tower of Pisa in Italy. The entire masterpiece is built at ratios of 1:1, 1:5 or 1:15. Though the Eiffel Tower of Paris is built at the ratio of one third, it is still 108 meters high. Tourists can go up to the tower top by observation elevator to have a panoramic view of Shenzhen and Hong Kong.

Chinese Gardens

Chinese Mausoleums

中国陵墓概述

After the emperors of the past dynasties seized the state power, the first and foremost thing for them to do was to build a resplendent and magnificent palace to show their dignity, and then, had their mausoleums built to show their power and prestige. However, as the mausoleums were underground, and the people could not feel the emperors' formidable power, the emperors paid great attention to the construction of the ground architectural structures of the mausoleum. The "height, large size, depth and solemnity" are the vital characteristics of the ground architectural structures of the Chinese mausoleums. In the Qin and Han dynasties (221 B.C.- A.D.220), the emperors had tall and large earth mausoleums built, and in the Tang Dynasty (618-907), the emperors had their mausoleums built in the mountains, emphasizing "height"; the mausoleum was usually surrounded by an inner wall, and an outer wall, which usually extended several dozens of kilometers, showing "large size"; from the first gate on the sacred road to the gate of the underground mausoleum stretched several kilometers, displaying "depth"; and the sacred road is lined by the ornamental columns, stone beasts, stone figures and stone tablets, implying "solemnity." The imperial mausoleums that make people feel solemnity and quietness are a scenic wonder in the ancient Chinese mausoleums.

Mausoleum of Yellow Emperor (New Stone Age: c. 10,000 to 4,000 years ago) – the Ancestral Tomb of the Chinese Nation

黄帝陵（新石器：约 10000—4000 年前）——中华民族的共同祖坟

❶

At the top of Qiaoshan Mountain, one kilometer north of the seat of Huangling County, Shaanxi Province in northwest China, it is the tomb of Xuanyuan, founder of the Chinese nation, known as "No. 1 mausoleum on earth. " The mausoleum is surrounded by mountains and rivers, and is covered with lushly growing pine and cypress forests. The mausoleum is 3.6 meters high, and 48 meters in circumference, encircled by a brick wall.

Since ancient times, the Mausoleum of Yel-

low Emperor is the symbol of the Chinese nation. At the Pure Brightness Festival (the fifth solar term) every year, the Chinese people from all over the world come here to pay respects to the ancestor of the Chinese nation. It has been a fine tradition of the Chinese people for thousands of years.

At the southeastern foot of Qiaoshan Mountain, the Temple of Yellow Emperor is where people offer sacrifices to and worship Yellow Emperor Xuanyuan. The temple was first built in the Han Dynasty (206 B.C.-A.D.220), and was renovated time and again in the following dynasties. An ancient cypress tree in the temple is 19 meters high and 10 meters in circumference. Legend has it that the tree was planted by Yellow Emperor in person; hence it has a history of over 5,000 years. Over 70 stone tablets inscribed with the funeral orations by the emperors of the past

❷

dynasties can be found in the temple. The Mausoleum of Yellow Emperor is a wonder in China's splendid history of civilization.

About Yellow Emperor (Huangdi)

黄帝简介:

Yellow Emperor was the common ancestor of all the ethnic groups in Central Plains at the end of the primitive society. His surname is Ji, and he styled himself Xuanyuan. Legend has it that Emperor Yan disturbed other tribes while Xuanyuan enjoyed the support of the all tribes. Later Yellow Emperor defeated Yan Emperor at Banquan (now the southeastern part of Zuolu in Hebei Province), and later the tribes led by Yellow Emperor killed Chiyou, a troublemaker, who was the chief of a large tribe in the east. Then Yellow Emperor became the leader of all the tribes.

It is also believed that there were many inventions originated from the time of Yellow Emperor. For instance, Yellow Emperor led his people to ex-

ploit the lower and middle reaches of the Yellow River; his wife Leizu taught people to grow mulberry trees, engage in sericulture and mend clothes by sewing; Cangjie, a high-ranking official, created pictographic characters; Danao worked out the calendar; Linglun made music instruments; and Leigong and Qibo made medicines. A medical book titled *Plain Questions* was written together by Huangdi, Qibo and Leigong, and is a part of a famous book *Huangdi's Internal Classic*. Many other inventions also originated from the time of Yellow Emperor, such as boats, carts, arrows, bows and numbers. The Chinese people call themselves "descendants of Yan and Huang" to this day. Here Yan and Huang refer to Yan Emperor and Yellow Emperor.

A saying goes that at the age of 110 (or 118), Yellow Emperor abandoned the throne and went to Mount Jin to cast a cauldron. On the day when the cauldron was accomplished, a yellow dragon came to issue an order from

❸

the Heavenly Emperor. Then Yellow Emperor got on the dragon, followed by over 70 officials. The dragon flew to the sky, and then descended at Qianshan Mountain, where Yellow Emperor said good-bye to his officials. Then the yellow dragon ascended to Heaven. To commemorate the merits and virtues of Yellow Emperor, the Chinese people buried his clothes, belts, boots and sword in Qianshan Mountain, which is the Mausoleum of Yellow Emperor. All the legends and historical records tell the Chinese people: Yellow Emperor is the founder of the Chinese nation, and a great inventor of the Chinese civilization.

① Qiaoshan Mountain
② Mausoleum of Yellow Emperor
③ Temple of Yellow Emperor
④ A stone sculpture of Yellow Emperor

❋ ❋ ❋ ❋ ❋ ❋ ❋ ❋

Mausoleum of Emperor Qin Shihuang (Qin Dynasty: 221-206 B.C.) – the Largest Mausoleum in the World

秦始皇陵(前221－前206)──世界上规模最大的陵墓

About 30 kilometers east of Xi'an in northwest China, the Mausoleum of Emperor Qin Shihuang is the largest mausoleum in the world. Soon after Emperor Qin Shihuang had ascended the throne at the age of 13, he began to have his mausoleum constructed. He died at 50 years old and was on the throne for 37 years. But it took him 36 years to have his mausoleum built. After he had annexed six ducal states, Emperor Qin Shihuang gathered 720,000 laborers to build his tomb for 11 years in succession. Originally, his tomb was over 100 meters high. After the weather erosion over the past 2,000-some years, the grave mound is now 47 meters high. Historical records describe the tomb as a magnificent underground city with an inner wall, 2,525.4 meters in circumference, and an outer wall, 6,264 meters in circumference. On the eastern side of the tomb, there are three vaults

two groups of painted bronze chariots and horses were excavated on the western side of the mausoleum; in August 1998, a large armor pit was discovered 150 meters southeast of the mausoleum, where a number of stone armors and stone helmets were excavated; and in May 1999, a large bronze cauldron with interlaced hydra design and two ears and pottery figures of actors was unearthed in the place 150 meters southeast of the mausoleum.

The Mausoleum of Emperor Qin Shihuang is now still a riddle. According to the information of the archaeological community of China, the underground palace where the emperor is buried has been well preserved. The Mausoleum of Emperor Qin Shihuang is included in the World Heritage List by the UNESCO.

that contain a great number of full-length terracotta warriors and horses, chariots and various kinds of weapons, totaling more than over 10,000 cultural relics. In December 1980,

About Emperor Qin Shihuang
秦始皇简介：

In 221 B.C., King Ying Zheng of the state of Qin conquered the states of Han, Yan, Wei, Chu and Qi, unified China and founded the first centralized feudal empire — the Qin Dynasty (221-207 B.C.). He considered his achievement surpassing the legendary "three emperors and five sovereigns," so he created a new title for himself "Huangdi (emperor)" together with "Shi (meaning the first)," hence he got the name Qin Shihuang (the First Emperor of the Qin Dynasty), hoping his descendants would follow in his steps to rule China for eternity. He unified the law, weights and measures, currency and the Chinese characters in writing; demolished the defensive works built by the former states during the Warring States period (475-221 B.C.); built

the roads to strengthen the national land communications; and ordered conscript laborers to link together the defensive works against marauding nomads. The adoption of all these measures promoted the prosperity and development of the economy and culture of the unified feudal country. To strengthen the ruling of the country, he ordered that all the folk weapons be destroyed; the history books of the former states and classics of Confucianism and various schools be burnt; and over 460 scholars who were not to his liking be killed. Emperor Qin Shihuang adopted feudal autocracy, cruel torture, tyranny, heavy exorbitant taxes and levies, and conscripted peasants for years running, making the people all over the country live a miserable life. Soon after his death, a large-scale peasant uprising broke out.

YangLing Mausoleum (Western Han: 206 B.C.-25 A.D.) – the First Fully Underground Mausoleum Museum in the World

汉阳陵(西汉：前 206－ 公元 25)───世界上第一座全地下现代化遗址博物馆

About 20 kilometers northwest of Xi'an City in northwest China, Yangling Mausoleum is where Liu Qi, the fourth emperor of the Western Han Dynasty (188 –141 B.C.), and his empress were buried. First constructed in 153 B.C., the graveyard covers an area of about 20 square kilometers. Archaeological researches prove that there are over 190 small tombs of other imperial family members,

nobles and officials in various sizes around the mausoleum. In 1998, archaeologists excavated 10 of the subsidiary tombs in a scientific way. On the basis of the period archaeological achievements, the Yangling Mausoleum Archaeological Exhibition Hall and the South Watchtower Gate Protection Hall were constructed; and in 2006, the Cultural Relics Protection and Exhibition Hall of the Yangling

Mausoleum was built. Visitors can see the cultural relics excavated from the 10 small tombs and the excavation environment, and how archaeological workers work and make excavation in the pits through the transparent glass under their feet and on both sides. It is a model of the reasonable combination of modern science & technology with the protection technology of cultural relics in China, as well as the first fully underground mausoleum museum in the world.

* * * * * * * * *

Qianling Mausoleum (Tang Dynasty: 618-907) – the Most Mysterious Joint Burial Place of Tang Emperor Gaozong and His Wife, Empress Wu Zetian, in China

乾陵(唐代:618—907)——中国最神秘的皇帝夫妻俩合葬墓

Located in Liangshan Mountain, six kilometers from the seat of Qianxian County, and about 75 kilometers northwest of Xi'an City in northwest China, it is a joint tomb of Emperor Gaozong and his wife Empress Wu Zetian, and the most representative tomb of all the mausoleums of the Tang Dynasty.

The mausoleum was built in line with the landform of the mountain, 1,047. 9 meters above sea level. According to the historical records, the mausoleum originally had two walls, the inner wall and outer wall, and watchtowers and huge stone carvings on the four sides. The ground stone carvings at the south gate have been basically well preserved, including a pair of ornamental columns, a pair of winged horses, a pair of ostriches, five pairs of saddled horses led by grooms, 10 pairs of stone generals with hats and gowns and holding swords, the Tablet Telling the Emperor's Deeds, the Uncharactered Tablet, and 61 stone statues of the chieftains of ethnic minorities and foreign envoys who came to Chang'an to attend the funeral rites of Emperor Gaozong. Each of the four gates of the inner city has a pair of large stone lions, which are vivid and lifelike stone carvings. Emperor Gaozong was buried in the Qianling Mausoleum

in the first year of the Wenming reign period (684); and Empress Wu Zetian was buried in the Qianling Mausoleum in the second year of the Shenlong reign period (706). To the southeast of the Qianling Mausoleum there are 17 attendants' tombs, of which five have been excavated, i.e., the tombs of Princess Yongtai Li Xian, Crown Prince Zhanghuai Li Xian, Crown Prince Yide Li Chongrun, Secretariat Director Xue Yuanchao and Right Guard General Li Jinxing. A great number of colorful murals, tricolor pottery figurines, stone outer coffins, stone gates, epitaphs and other important cultural relics have been ex-

cavated from their tombs.

The Qianling Mausoleum has not been excavated; hence the mausoleum is still a riddle to us. In 1958, the archaeological workers of China made a research into the tomb and found the tomb paths and trenches all built of flagstones, which are fixed by iron board and filled with iron pulp. There are 18 mausoleums of the Tang emperors in Guangzhong Area in Shaanxi, of which 17 were robbed. *The History of the Five Dynasties . Biography of Wen Tao* tells: Wen Tao robbed many imperial tombs of the Tang Dynasty. When digging the Qianling Mausoleum, he failed

because of the heavy rain and strong wind. The archaeological investigation also proves that the Qianling Mausoleum has never been robbed in history.

The Qianling Mausoleum is the only joint tomb for an emperor and an empress in China, who were a couple. Before his death, Emperor Gaozong of the Tang Dynasty left his last words that all his favorite books, brushes and ink sticks be placed in his tomb, indicating that the Qianling Mausoleum must hold abundant cultural relics. It can be predicted that the excavation of the mausoleum will find it a huge and splendid underground cultural relics warehouse.

About Emperor Gaozong and Empress Wu Zetian 唐高宗、武则天简介:

Emperor Gaozong Li Zhi (628-683) was the ninth son of Emperor Taizong and the third emperor of the Tang Dynasty. He was on the throne from 649-684, and named Wu Zetian his empress in the sixth year of the Yonghui reign period. In the fifth year of the Xianqing reign period (660), Emperor Gaozong fell ill, and Empress Wu began to participate in state affairs. From then on, Empress Wu became more and more powerful with the passage of time. After Emperor Gaozong passed away, Wu Zetian took the throne herself and titled her reign "Zhou," becoming the first empress in Chinese history to rule the country.

Wu Zetian (624-705) was the empress of Gaozong and Empress of the "Wuzhou" empire. She was on the throne from 690 to 705, the only female monarch in Chinese history. At the age of fourteen, Wu Zetian became a concubine to Emperor Taizong. She was given the title Cairen (a fifth grade concubine of the Tang Dynasty). When she was waiting upon Emperor Taizong who was sick, she committed adultery with Crown Prince Li Zhi. After the death of Taizong, Wu Zetian,

❸

❹

aged 26, and all the other emperors' concubines were sent to the Ganye Temple to live out their days. In 652, Emperor Gaozong summoned Wu Zetian to the palace and doted on her. In 654, he named Wu Zetian Zhaoyi (the second grade concubine of the new emperor). In the sixth year of the Yonghui reign period (655), Wu Zetian, 32, was named the empress. In his late years, Emperor Gaozong was seriously sick, and Empress Wu Zetian took an active part in state affair. She would appear in court alongside the emperor whenever he held an audience. The pair became known as the Holy Sovereigns. After the death of Gaozong, Wu Zetian suddenly broke with usual practice and deposed Emperor Zhongzong in 684, and later Emperor Ruirong. At the age of 60, Wu Zetian usurped the throne, called herself Holy Empress and declared the empire was henceforth ruled by

the Zhou Dynasty, which was called Wuzhou in history. Wu Zetian was on the throne for 21 years. In 705, Emperor Zhongzong restored the Tang Dynasty to power, and Wu Zetian moved to Luoyang and enjoyed the title "Zetian Holy Empress." Aged 82, Wu Zetian died in December 705 in Luoyang. In 706, she was buried alongside Emperor Gaozong in Qianling Mausoleum.

① Stone animals on the Sacred Way
② Qianling Mausoleum
③ Tomb of Princess Yongtai
④ The colorful murals in the Tomb of Crown Prince Zhanghuai
⑤ Uncharactered Tablet
⑥ A stone general on the Sacred Way

Ming Tombs (Ming: 1368-1644) – the Best-Preserved Imperial Tombs in China

明十三陵(明代:1368-1644)———中国保存最完整的帝王陵墓群

Lying at the foot of Tianshou Mountain in Changping District, about 45 kilometers north of Beijing, the Ming tombs are spread over an area of 40 square kilometers and include the tombs of the 13 Ming emperors, namely, Changling, Xianling, Jingling, Yuling, Maoling, Tailing, Kangling, Yongling, Zhaoling, Dingling, Qingling, Deling and Siling. Hence the necropolis is known as Thirteen Tombs. Construction of the tombs lasted more than 200 years, starting from the seventh year(1409) of the Yongle reign period of the Ming Dynasty when the construction of Changling Mausoleum started, to the first year (1644) of the Shunzhi reign period of the Qing Dynasty when the construction of Siling Mausoleum was completed. The Ming Dynasty had 16 emperors and ruled China for 276 years. The first emperor of the Ming Dynasty, Zhu Yuanzhang, made Nanjing his capital, and was buried in Xiaoling Mausoleum in Nanjing. Two emperors of the Ming Dynasty fought with each other for the throne, resulting in that one was missing, and the other was buried in some other place.

The necropolis of the Ming tombs is surrounded by mountains in the east, west and north, and on the southern side stand Dragon and Tiger mountains, which are like a natural gate guarded by a dragon and a tiger. Each mausoleum lies at the foot of a mountain, and all of the tombs are linked by a "Sacred Way," forming a huge whole with a distinction between the major and minor ones. The necropolis was encircled by walls; and had two palace gates, one large and the other small, and 10 passes. Each pass had a fortress building guarded by imperial troops. Most of the walls and buildings have already collapsed. The Ming tombs are close to Beijing, and the underground architectural structures are very solid and deep. Hence they have never been robbed. The Ming tombs are the best-pre-

3

❷

served imperial tombs in China.

The Sacred Way of the Ming Tombs 十三陵神道 symbolizes the guard of honor of the emperor during his lifetime. The Sacred Way stretches 750 meters long and is lined by 24 stone animals, i.e., lions, *xiezhi* (mythical beasts), elephants, camels, *qilin* (mythical beasts) and horses, which are followed by 12 stone human figures, including four military officials, four civil officials and four meritorious officials. The practice of placing stone animals and stone human figures before imperial tombs symbolizes that *yin* and *yang* (two opposing principles in nature) alternate day and night, and animals and military and civil officials guard the soul of the deceased emperors day and night, to show the consolidation of the dynasty.

The Changling 长陵，which lies at the foot of the main peak of Tianshou Mountain, is the tomb of Emperor Chengzu Zhu Di of the Ming Dynasty and his empress. The first and biggest tomb of the 13 Ming tombs, it was constructed in the 11th year of the Yongle reign period (1413) of the Ming Dynasty. Sixteen concubines of the emperor who were the victims of the cruel practice of burying the living with the dead were also buried in the tomb. The mausoleum is surrounded by walls, and is divided into three courtyards, including the gate, Stele Pavilion, Hall of Prominent Favor (Ling'endian) and Baocheng (Precious City). Of them, the Hall of Prominent Favor is the most magnificent, where sacrifices were offered to the deceased emperor. With an area of 1,956 square meters, the hall contains 60 *nanmu* (a fine hardwood) pillars, with a diameter of 1.17 meters and 14.3 height at maximum. Such a large and gorgeous *nanmu* building that is as solid as before after more than 500 years is the only one of such kind in China. The underground palace of the

Changling has not been excavated yet.

The Dingling 定陵 is the first tomb of the 13 Ming tombs that was excavated. Located on the western side of Tianshou Mountain, the Dingling is the tomb of Zhu Yijun and his two empresses Xiaoduan and Xiaojing. The location of the Dingling was chosen by Zhu Yijun himself when he was on the throne. The construction of the tomb began in the 12th year of the Wanli reign period (1584) of the Ming Dynasty when Zhu Yijun was a young man of 22. It took six years to complete in the 18th year of the Wanli reign period (1590).

The excavation of the Dingling started in May 1956, and it took one whole year for the Chinese archaeologists to find the entrance. More than 3,000 cultural relics were excavated from the tomb, including silk fabrics, and gold, silver, jade and porcelain wares,

❹

■ Chinese Mausoleums

⑤

On both sides of the coffins are 26 red lacquered wooden boxes filled with precious funeral objects and pieces of jade and blue-and-white porcelain wares.

The two annexes have the same layout, and contain nothing inside. According to the opinions of the relevant experts, the annexes of the underground palace of the Dingling were originally built for the two empresses. But when the coffins were being transported to the underground palace, it was found that the passageways to the annexes were too narrow to go through. Consequently the coffins of empresses had to be placed in the rear hall. It is an extraordinary case.

which represent the highest craftsmanship of the Ming Dynasty. The cultural relics excavated from the tomb are on display at the eastern and western exhibition halls for visitors to appreciate.

The underground palace consists of five spacious halls: an antechamber, central hall, rear hall and right and left annexes. The vaulted halls are built with stones, 27 meters deep, 87.34 meters long and 47.28 meters wide, and have a floor space of 1,195 square meters. The underground palace has a total of seven marble stone gates, and each is 3.3 meters high, and 1.8 meters wide and weighs about four tons.

At the central hall are three white marble thrones. In front of each throne is a blue-and-white porcelain tub of oil, with the "everlasting lamp." The lamp was light when the emperor was buried, but after the tomb was closed, the flame soon died for want of oxygen.

The rear hall is the main part of the underground palace. In the center is a dais on which is placed the coffin of Emperor Zhu Yijun, with the coffins containing Empress Xiaoduan on his left and Empress Xiaojing on his right.

The 13 Ming tombs in the necropolis, which vary in size and fastidiousness, are similar in the layout and specifications. The rectangle tombs all include the same ground architectures, such as the gate, Stele Pavilion, Gate of Prominent Favor (Ling'enmen), Hall of Prominent Favor, Visible Tower (Minglou) and Precious City. Now the Ming Tombs has been included in the World Heritage List by the UNESCO.

① Changling Tomb
② Sacred Way of the Ming Tombs
③ Underground Palace of the Dingling
④ Hall of Prominent Favor
⑤ Xianling Tomb

Eastern Tombs of the Qing Dynasty (Qing: 1644-1911) – the Largest and the Most Complete Group of Imperial Tombs in China

清东陵(清代:1644—1911)——中国现存规模最大的帝王陵墓群

Located in Malanyu in Zunhua City in north China, the necropolis is about 125 kilometers east of Beijing, hence the name Eastern Tombs. It is one of the sites of the imperial tombs of the Qing Dynasty after Beijing was named the capital of the country. Another group of the imperial tombs in Yixian County, Hebei Province, to the west of Beijing is called

1

Chinese Mausoleums

the Western Tombs. The Qing Dynasty is the last feudal society in China that lasted 268 years. The 10 emperors of the Qing Dynasty were buried in the Eastern and Western tombs, respectively. Now the Eastern Tombs are the largest and the most complete group of imperial tombs in China.

The necropolis contains five tombs for the Qing emperors, i.e., Xiaoling (Shunzhi), Yuling (Qianlong), Dingling (Xianfeng) and Huiling (Tongzhi), four tombs for the empresses, five tombs for concubines and one tomb for princesses. Altogether five emperors, 15 empresses and over 130 concubines of the Qing Dynasty were buried here. The construction of the Eastern Tombs started in the 18th year of the Shunzhi reign period (1661) of the Qing Dynasty. With Changrui Mountain as the center, the necropolis is about 12.5 kilometers from south to north, and about 20 kilometers from east to west. The 15 tombs lie

❸

and about five kilometers long. Along the Sacred Way, visitors can find the stone memorial archways, Great Red Gate, Greater Stele Pavilion with a stele inscribed with an account of the accomplishments of the deceased Shunzhi, stone human figures, Dragon and Phoenix Gate, bridges and stele pavilions, eastern and western waiting rooms, duty offices and side chambers, Hall of Eminent Favor (Long'endian), three gates, two pillar gates, stone sacrificial altars, Visible Tower, Precious City and Precious Dome. Under the Precious Dome is the underground place, where the coffins are placed.

at the southern foot of Changrui Mountain, with undulating hills in the east and west. In front of the tombs is an open country with an area of nearly 50 square kilometers. The Xiaoling occupies the central position below the main peak of Changrui Mountain and is flanked by other tombs, with crisscrossed sacred ways and bridges. All the architectural structures are roofed with yellow and green glazed tiles, and have painted pillars and red walls, forming a quiet and magnificent picture.

The Sacred Way in the Eastern Tombs 清东陵神道 is in the south of the mausoleum. Paved with bricks, the Sacred Way leads from a huge archway to the Precious Dome of the Xiaoling, 12 meters wide

Underground Palace of the Yuling (Tomb of Emperor Qianlong) Mausoleum 裕陵（乾隆墓）地宫 is to the west of the Xiaoling. It is 54 meters long and covers a total floor space of 327 square meters. The vaulted underground palace has four double doors all of stone. Each door is a carving of a Bodhisattva, all of them different in expression and pose. The inner walls, arched chamber ceilings and gateways are all carved with Buddhist statues, patterns and scriptures, hence it is like a grand underground hall for worshipping Buddha. The underground palace is by far the largest and finest among the Eastern Tombs, showing the magnificent architecture and a high technical level.

4

① Yuling Mousoleum
② The Eastern Tombs of the Qing Dynasty
③ The Sacred Way
④ The indoor scene of the Underground Palace

Sun Yat-sen Mausoleum (Republic of China: 1911-1949) – the Largest Mausoleum in Modern Chinese History

中山陵(民国：1911−1949)————中国近代史上的最大陵墓

Situated on the southern slope of Zhongshan Mountain in the eastern suburbs of Nanjing in east China, it is the mausoleum of Dr. Sun Yat-sen, the great forerunner of China's democratic revolution. On March 12, 1925, Sun Yat-sen passed away in Beijing. According to his last wish, the construction of the mausoleum started in January 1926, and was completed in the spring of 1929. On June 1, 1929, Dr. Sun's remains were moved here from the Temple of Azure Clouds in Beijing by the National Government. The whole project of the Sun Yat-sen Mausoleum was basically completed in 1933.

The mausoleum, which was designed by Lü Yanzhi, a famous architect, is in the pattern of an "alarm bell," expressing Dr. Sun's wish the masses of the people would be aroused. Sheltered by hill slopes and built in line with the landform of the mountain, the mausoleum faces the south, and consists of a square, memorial archways, a tomb passage, a stele pavilion, a memorial hall and a coffin chamber. A copper statue of Dr. Sun Yat-sen stands in the square. From the entrance of the tomb passage to the coffin chamber totals over 700 meters long, with 397 steps. The whole mausoleum is imposing and magnificent.

In the center of the memorial hall is a marble-stone sitting statue of Dr. Sun Yat-sen, which is surrounded by relief sculptures describing Dr. Sun's revolutionary deeds. On the walls of the memorial hall is inscribed his posthumous work "The Grand Outline for the Construction of the Nation." Behind the memorial hall is the coffin chamber, in the center of which is a round marble stone pit, with a rectangle coffin in the center. A prostrate marble statue of Sun is on the coffin, and the remains of Dr. Sun Yat-sen lie in the tomb in composure.

The Sun Yat-sen Mausoleum covers an area of 1.3 million square meters, and the tomb passageway is flanked by evergreen pine and cypress trees, and the tomb is surrounded by green mountains. The mausoleum faces an open country, and backs on to a towering peak. The architectural layout and shape display the traditional Chinese national style. Hence it is a wonder in China's modern mausoleums.

About Dr. Sun Yat-sen 孙中山简介：

Sun Yat-sen (Nov. 12,1866-Mar. 12, 1925) is a great democratic revolutionary of modern China. His name is Wen, and he styled himself Yixian. A native of Xiangshan County (present-day Zhongshan City) in Guangdong Province, he graduated from the College of Medicine for Chinese in Hong Kong in the 18th year of the Guangxu reign period (1892) of the Qing Dynasty, and then practiced medi-

cine in Macao and Guangzhou. In 1894, he submitted a petition to Li Hongzhang, proposing that China carry out reforms to bring about independence and prosperity, but his proposal was turned down. Then he went to Honolulu where he founded the Society to Restore China's Prosperity (Xing Zhong Hui), and put forward the slogan of "rejuvenating China." In 1905, he founded the Chinese Revolutionary League (Tong Men Hui) in Tokyo, Japan, and was elected premier. The league put forward the political program to "expel the Manchus, restore China, establish a republic and equalize land rights." Soon afterwards, Sun summed up the league's program as the Three People's Principles — the principle of nationalism, the principle of democracy, and the principle of people's livelihood. On October 11, 1911, the Wuchang Uprising won a success, and the uprising army founded the Military Government, which was followed by the founding of the Republic of China. On December 29, Sun Yat-sen was elected Provisional President of the Republic of China. On January 1, 1912, Sun Yat-sen was inaugurated in Nanjing and announced the founding of the Republic of China, thus putting an end to the feudal autocratic monarchy that had ruled China for over 2,000 years as well as the Qing Dynasty that had ruled China for 260-some years.

Chinese Mausoleums

Chinese Buddhist Temples 中国佛寺概述

Along with the introduction of Buddhism to China, Buddhist temples sprang up like mushrooms throughout the country. Legend has it that in the Eastern Han Dynasty (25-220), two monks from the Western Regions, by the name Kashyapa-matanga and Dharmaranya, came to Luoyang, the capital of China, to take charge of the translation of the sutras. The court had an official residence outside of the west gate of Luoyang renovated for the two eminent monks to live, and translate and store the sutras. This house was the earliest Buddhist temple in China. Legend goes that as the sutras were carried to the temple by a white horse, the emperor named it White Horse Temple.

In the early days, the Chinese Buddhist temples were located in densely populated capital cities for convenience of preaching Buddhism. Later along with the development of Buddhism, temples were gradually built in the picturesque mountains with exquisite waters where monks can cultivate themselves through meditation, giving birth to the situation that "most of the famous mountains are occupied by monks." Mount Wutai in Shanxi, Mount Putuo in Zhejiang, Mount Jiuhua in Anhui and Mount Emei in Sichuan are the four most famous Buddhist mountains in China, which are still shining the splendid brilliance of Buddhist culture today.

Though Buddhism was born in India, it became flourishing in China. No one knows how many temples China has built since ancient times. It is said that in the period from the Western Jin Dynasty (265-317) to the end of the Tang Dynasty (618-907), China had over 100,000 temples; a large temple had over 500 monks; and the largest temple held 10,000 monks. Though numerous temples were destroyed with the passage of time or in the war, a great number of Buddhist temples have been preserved. In 1949 when New China was founded, China had a total of over 5,000 temples spread all over the country.

Chinese Buddhist temples show strong national independence. Their huge architectural scale, the beautiful Buddhist statues and the colorful murals with rich contents make all the Chinese people feel proud, and all the people in the world gasp in admiration.

Mount Wutai (Eastern Han-Ming: 68-1644) – the Most Famous Buddhist Mountain in China

五台山(东汉 – 明代：公元 68–1644)——中国最著名的佛教名山

Located in Wutai County, Shanxi Province in central China, Mount Wutai (meaning Five Platforms) is one of the four famous Buddhist mountains in China. As its name indicates, Mount Wutai is surrounded by five peaks with the tops as flat as five platforms. The five peaks are 250 kilometers in circumference. It is not hot in summers, hence another name Cool Mountain. With Taihuai Town as the center, Mount Wutai covers an area of 2,837

known as Sakyamuni Stupa, is a Tibetan-style dagoba. Standing at the Tayuan Monastery in Taihuai Town in Mount Wutai, the circular dagoba is 54.27 meters high. This dagoba is beautifully shaped, thick alternating with thin, and square matching round. A total of 252 bells hung from the edge of the plate jingle pleasantly in the breeze, showing a character of an ancient dagoba. It is regarded as the signpost of Mount Wutai.

Prominence Temple (Xiantongsi) 显通寺 in Taihuai Town in Mount Wutai covers an area of 80,000 square meters, and includes 400 halls, buildings and monks' dormitories, all of which were built in the Ming and Qing dynasties. The temple was first constructed in the Yongping reign period (58-75) of the Eastern Han Dynasty. Like the White Horse Temple in Luoyang, it is one of the oldest temples in China. Legend has it that once Bodhisattva of Wisdom preached Buddhism here, and now it is well known for the Immeasurable Hall, Bronze Hall, bronze pagodas and other bronze cultural relics. The Bronze Hall was first con-

square kilometers.

Buddhism in Mount Wutai has a long history. As early as in the 11th year of the Yongping reign period (68) of the Eastern Han Dynasty, construction of Buddhist temples started. After the expansion and renovation of the temples in the following dynasties, now 47 temples built in the dynasties after the Tang (619-907) have been preserved, making Mount Wutai enjoy the reputation of being an ancient architecture warehouse in China. The temples in the mountain include Han Buddhist temples, as well as Tibetan Buddhist monasteries. Hence it is the best place for the people to study China's ancient architecture, religions, culture and art.

Legend has it that Mount Wutai was the place of enlightenment of Manjusri (Bodhisattva of Wisdom). On the fourth day of the fourth lunar month every year, the birthday of Manjusri, all the monks of the temples in the mountain chant scriptures and hold religious service, which attract numerous domestic and foreign tourists to do sightseeing and worship Buddha.

Large White Dagoba 大白塔, also

structed in the 37th year of the Wanli reign period (1609) of the Ming Dynasty, five meters high. It is said that over one million *jin* (one *jin* = 0.5 kilogram) of bronze was collected from 10,000 families of the 13 provinces to build this hall. The hall has double eaves and a roof in *xieshan* style (a traditional style of Chinese palace architecture, fully pilled on both sides, and half-hipped at the ends, so that an upper gable is left exposed). The four-side upper story has six doors, and the four-side lower story has eight doors, each door decorated with beautiful flower patterns. The whole bronze hall is majestically decorated and exquisitely cast. This bronze building is rare in China.

The Nanchan Temple Hall 南禅寺大殿 is on the western side of Lijiazhuang, 22 kilometers southwest of the seat of Wutai County in Shanxi Province. It was first con-

structed in the Tang Dynasty (618-907), with the exact date unknown. An inscription under a beam at the hall proves that it was rebuilt in the third year of the Jianzhong reign period (782) of the Tang Dynasty. In the late Tang, most of the Buddhist temples in the country were destroyed due to the policy adopted by Emperor Wuzong, known as the "religious persecutions during the Huichang reign period." As the Nanchan Temple is in an out-of-the-way place, it escaped by sheer luck. Now it is the oldest wooden architecture in China, a wonder among China's ancient architectural structures.

The Nanchan Temple Hall has a Buddhist altar, which is covered with color sculptures. The statue of Sakyamuni is in the center, with 17 sculptures of his disciples, Bodhisattvas, heavenly kings, and celestial boys on both sides and in the front. Each of them has a

⑤

plump face and a natural expression, and wears simple clothes with smooth patterns. They are masterpieces of the ancient Chinese painted sculptures. With a history of over 1,200 years, these color sculptures have been well preserved, a wonder indeed.

The Eastern Hall of the Buddha's Halo Temple 佛光寺东大殿is on the slope halfway up the mountain, about 32 kilometers northeast of Shanxi Province. The temple lushly grows pine and cypress trees and boasts a clean and quiet environment. First constructed in the Emperor Xiaowen reign period (471-499) of the Northern Wei Dynasty, the temple became prosperity in the Sui and Tang dynasties when its influence reached Japan. In the fifth year of the Huichang reign period (845) of the Tang Dynasty, Emperor Wuzong banned Buddhism and many Buddhist temples were destroyed. After Emperor Xuanzong ascended to the throne, Buddhism

was restored. The temple was rebuilt in the 11th year of the Dazhong reign period (857). The Eastern Hall in the temple is large and magnificent, integrating wooden structures, sculptures, murals and paintings, and is the only and invaluable building of such kind, and a wonder among the ancient architectural structures of the Tang Dynasty. It occupies an important position in the world architecture history. On the Buddhist altar in the Eastern Hall stand 35 color sculptures of the Tang Dynasty. The color sculptures feature pump faces, smooth lines and natural and well-proportioned bodies. They are masterpieces of color sculptures of the Tang Dynasty.

---

① Mount Wutai and Large White Dagoba
② Bronze Hall
③ Nanchan Temple
④ Eastern Hall of the Buddha's Halo Temple
⑤ A group of color sculptures in the Buddha's Halo Temple

Shaolin Temple (Northern Wei-Present: 386-Present) – the Origin of the Chinese Martial Arts

少林寺(北魏至今：386至今)——中国武功的发源地

Lying at the northern foot of Shaoshi Mountain, a range of Mt. Songshan, 13 kilometers northwest of Dengfeng City, over 100 kilometers west of Zhengzhou in Henan Province in central China, the Shaolin Temple was first constructed in the 19th year of the Taihe reign period (495) of the Northern Wei Dynasty. An eminent monk from India took a long way to China to preach Buddhism. Emperor Xiaowen, a believer of Buddhism, had a temple built in the forest of Shaoshi Mountain, and named it Shaolin Temple. In the third year of the Xiaochang reign period (527) of the Northern Wei, an Indian monk

❶

2

Bodhidharma came here and founded Chan sect of Buddhism. Hence in history, Bodhidharma was named the founder of Chan sect, and Shaolin Temple was known as the ancestral temple. In the early Tang Dynasty, the monks of the Shaolin Temple helped Emperor Taizong with the founding of the Tang Dynasty. Since then, it has been a routine that the monks in the temple practice martial arts everyday. The Chan sect and Shaolin martial arts have enjoyed a high reputation and have been spread far and wide. In the Tang Dynasty (618-907), the temple had about 2,500 monks in total. In the 16th century, the monks of the Shaolin Temple, who were good at practicing martial arts, once defeated foreign pirates. As a result, the temple was funded by the emperors for several hundred years, and became one of the most famous temples in China. As the Shaolin Temple has played an important role in the development and dissemination of Chinese martial arts, it is known as "No. 1 Temple on Earth." Chinese martial arts are well known because of the Shaolin Temple; and in return, the Shaolin Temple enjoys a worldwide reputation because of Chinese martial arts. The Shaolin Temple is not only the sacred land of Buddhism, but also a place worshipped by Chinese and foreign martial arts lovers.

Standing-on-Snow Pavilion 立雪亭 in the Shaolin Temple was originally known as Dharma Pavilion. Legend has it that one night, a disciple by the name Shen Guang came to Dharma Pavilion for advice in spite of heavy snow. When seeing Master Dharma sit in meditation in the room, he dared not to disturb him. His two knees were covered with snow, but Shen Guang still stood in the open area, putting the palms together before him.

Chinese Buddhist Temples

Dharma walked out of the room after finishing his meditation, and asked: "Why are you standing in the snow?" Shen Guang replied after wiping off his tears: "I came here to ask Master for advice on Buddhist doctrines." Dharma kept silent for a while and then said: "I would take you as my disciple unless there was a fall of red snow." Upon hearing it, Shen Guang understood the implied meaning. He drew a monk's knife with his right hand, and cut off his left arm, with blood falling down on white snow. Master Dharma lost no time to wrap Shen Guang's injured arm with his kasaya, and tied a knot at the waist. The kasaya turned red in a moment. Finding Shen Guang was in great sincerity with a will of steel, Dharma named him Hui Ke and taught him Buddhist doctrines, and gave his mantle, alms and religious ritual implements to Hui Ke. As Hui Ke learnt well the doctrines of Chan sect, and received the things left by Master Dharma, he inherited and developed Chan sect of Buddhism. Later he was named the "second ancestor of Chan sect." Halfway up Shaoshi Mountain stands the Second Ancestor's Hut, where Hui Ke once stood in

❸

Chinese Buddhist Temples ▮

snow and cut off his arm. To commemorate the two founders of Buddhism and the extraordinary event, the monks of the Shaolin Temple named it "Standing-on-Snow Pavilion," made a blood-red kasaya and draped it over the left shoulder of the statue to vividly show how Dharma wrapped Hui Ke's injured arm with kasaya. This story has been handed down generation by generation, symbolizing the absolute sincerity of the monks in believing Buddhism.

Shaolin Boxing Murals 少林寺拳谱壁画 on the north and south walls of the White Clothing Hall at the Shaolin Temple show lots of monks practicing martial arts with or without apparatuses. The murals truly record the Shaolin Temple's history of practicing martial arts in the Ming Dynasty (1368-1644).

Pitfalls, commonly known as "foot pits," were left on the ground of the Thousand Buddha Hall of the Shaolin Temple by the monks when practicing martial arts.

The Forest of Pagodas 塔林, about 300 meters west of the Shaolin Temple, is the graveyard of the monks of the past dynasties. Now it contains 220-some brick and stone pagodas built from the Tang Dynasty to the Qing Dynasty (618-1911). The pagodas were built in the different dynasties, so that each shows its unique shape. Most pagodas have carvings and inscriptions. Hence the Forest of Pagodas is a treasure-house for the research on Chinese ancient architecture and carving art, and is a great wonder in the Chinese tomb pagoda history.

① Shaollin Temple
② Standing-on-Snow Pavilion
③ The Forest of Pagodas
④ One of the *Shaolin Boxing Murals*

Dule Temple (Tang: 618-907) – a Clay Buddhist Statue That Did Not Collapse in Earthquakes

独乐寺(唐代：618—907)——地震震不倒的泥菩萨

In the seat of Jixian County in the western suburbs of Tianjin in north China, the Dule Temple is about 100 kilometers from Tianjin, and about 90 kilometers west of Beijing. Legend has it that it was the place where An Lushan, a local official in charge of the military and administrative affairs of several pre-

fectures in the Tang Dynasty, held a rally to pledge resolution before rising in rebellion. As he was fond of enjoying happiness by himself rather than with other people, it was named Dule (Enjoying Happiness by Oneself) Temple. The gate of the temple and the Avalokitesvara Pavilion rebuilt in the second

year of the Tonghe reign period (984) of the Liao Dynasty are the representative works of the Chinese ancient wood-structure architecture. The Avalokitesvara Pavilion, 23 meters high, is the oldest wood-structure and multi-story tower. It has experienced 28 earthquakes, including three destructive earthquakes, but the pavilion stands still when all the surrounding buildings all collapsed. It is a wonder in Chinese ancient architecture! The more interesting is that a statue of Avalokitesvara in the pavilion, which is 16 meters high and is the highest painted clay statue in China, has been well preserved in the past 1,000 years or so. It is a wonder among wonders.

Suspended Temple (Ming and Qing: 1368-1911) – the Buddhist Temple Hung in the Air

悬空寺(明清：1368—1911)——挂在半空中的佛寺

The Suspended Temple, which is five kilometers south of the seat of Hunyuan County and about 90 kilometers south of Datong in Shanxi Province in central China, is built halfway up the mountainous cliffs. The historical records reveal that the temple was first con-

structed in the late Northern Wei (c. the sixth century), and the present architecture was rebuilt in the Ming and Qing dynasties (1368-1911).

Built halfway up the mountain, the temple has dangerous precipices above and a deep valley down, like hanging in the mid-air. It is a rare ancient architecture suspended in the air in China. A local saying goes: "Suspended Temple hung by three horsetails in the mid-air." The temple has 40 halls, towers and pavilions, which are all wood-structure architectural structures, supported with flying beams inserted into the cliffs and wooden pillars and connected by winding corridors by cleverly using the mechanic principle. The temple holds nearly 80 bronze, iron, stone and clay statues. The more interesting is that in the Three Religions Hall, the statues of Sakyamuni, Lao Zi and Confucius are worshipped in the same hall, showing the great harmony between Buddhism, Taoism and Confucianism, and displaying the designer's broad-mindedness. In the Tang Dynasty (618-907), Li Bai, a famous poet, once paid a visit to Mount Hengshan, and wrote an inscription, meaning "magnificence," which was inscribed on the northern cliff, adding much radiance to the temple.

✳   ✳   ✳   ✳   ✳   ✳   ✳   ✳

Tashilhunpo Monastery (Ming: 1368-1644) – a Temple with the Buddhist Statue Closest to Heaven

扎什伦布寺(明代：1368—1644)——有离天庭最近的大佛

Lying at the foot of Nyiseri Mountain in south Xigaze, Tibet in southwest China, the Tashilhunpo Monastery means the "Auspicious Sumeru." Founded by the First Dalai Lama, Gendun Drup, who was a disciple of Tsongkhapa, founder of Gelug (Yellow) Sect, it has been the religious and political center of the Panchen lamas after the fourth Panchen took in charge of the monastery. Built in line with the landform of the mountain, the monastery has a floor space of 300,000 square meters, 14 gold tops in various sizes, 56 sutra halls in different sizes, and layer upon layer of palaces laid out in the fashion of a maze. Looking from a distance, the Tashilhunpo Monastery is just like a town, so that it is a great wonder among the Tibetan Buddhist architectural structures. The stupa tombs of Panchen lamas of the past ages are located in the monastery. Covered with silver pieces and

inlaid with various kinds of precious stones, the stupa tombs are brilliant and glistering. The monastery also collects a great number of Buddhist statues, *Tangka* 唐卡 (traditional Tibetan paintings), embroideries, and various kinds of beautiful and precious cultural relics, sacrificial vessels and porcelain wares. Among the valuable cultural relics in the monastery are a great number of gold and jade seals,

the imperial edicts on conferring titles for the successive Panchen lamas issued by the emperors of the Ming and Qing dynasties, and the "seal of Minister of Education" in Phagpa script of the Yuan Dynasty. All these are important data for the study of the ancient culture of Tibet and the history of the relationship between Tibet and Han.

The Great Champa Buddha Hall 大强巴佛殿 is on the western side of the Tashilhunpo Monastery. The construction of the hall started by the Ninth Panchen, Choji Nyingma, in 1904, and lasted four years. The hall has a floor space of 862 square meters, and is 30 meters high. A large bronze statue of Champa Buddha — Maitreya (Buddha of the Future, who is called Champa Buddha in the Tibetan language) stands in the hall. The Buddhist statue is 22.7 meters tall and sits on a 3.8-meter-high terrace, totaling 26.7 meters high. The Buddha's middle finger is 1.2

meters long; his foot is 4.2 meters long; his shoulder is 11.5 meters wide; and his ear is 2.2 meters long. According to the historical records, a fine long hair between the brows of the Buddhist statue is made of a diamond as large as a walnut, 30 diamonds in the size of broad beans, over 300 pearls and more than 1,400 corals, ambers and other precious stones. It took 110 artisans' four years to finish casting it by using 558 *jin* (one *jin* = 0.5 kilogram) of gold and over 230,000 *jin* of red copper. At that time the productivity was very low. Under such bad conditions, the casting of such a huge and beautiful Buddhist statue is a marvel created by the Tibetan people.

The Stupa of the 10th Panchen Lama 十世班禅祀殿灵塔 is in the west of the Tashilhunpo Monastery. The construction of the Memorial Hall of the 10th Panchen Lama was finished in 1993. The hall is about 35 meters high, and includes a gold stupa, which is 11.52 meters high, covered by gold and inlaid with precious stones. The building of the stupa cost over 400 kilograms of gold, and it is the largest gold stupa in China. The remains of the 10th Panchen Lama are laid in the stupa. It is the first gold stupa built by the Chinese government for a religious leader.

Chinese Buddhist Temples

Yonghe Lamasery (Qing: 1644-1911) with a Famous Giant Sandalwood Buddha

雍和宫（清代：1644-1911）——有著名的顶天立地的檀木大佛

Located in Beijing, the Yonghe Palace was first constructed in the 33rd year of the Kangxi reign period (1694) of the Qing Dynasty, and was turned into a lamasery in the ninth year of the Qianlong reign period (1744), which later became the Qing government's administration center for national affairs related to Lamaism. With an area of 66,400 square meters, the Yonghe Lamasery contains five main halls, i.e., Heavenly King Hall, Main Hall, Hall of Everlasting Protection, Hall of the Wheel of the Law and Pavilion of Ten Thousand Happiness. The Yonghe Lamasery is an architectural complex showing the characteristics of the Tibetan, Han, Mongolia and Manchu ethnic groups. Each hall preserves thousands of Buddhist statues and Buddhist classical cultural relics.

The front part of the lamasery is open and wide, and the back half is dense and undulating, and halls and pavilions with up-turned eaves and crisscrossed ridges are laid out in the fashion of a maze. It is the largest and most gorgeous lamasery of Gelug Sect of Tibetan Buddhism in the inland.

The Hall of Wheel of the Law 法轮殿, in the shape of a cross, has five small pavilions on the roof covered with glazed tiles, and on each pavilion stands a small tiny lama pagoda. On the altar in the hall is a bronze statue, six meters high, of Master Tsongkhapa. At the rear of the altar is the elaborate "Mountain of 500 Arhats." Tsongkahapa was born in Xining Prefecture, Qinghai in the 15th year of the Yongle reign (1417) of the Ming Dynasty. He left home and became a monk at the age of 14 and is the founder of Yellow Sect of Lamaism. The Hall of Wheel of the Law is the place where lamas hold Buddhist services, as well as the crystallization of the Han and Tibetan culture and art.

The Pavilion of Ten Thousand Happiness 万福阁, also known as the Hall of Great Buddha, is the tallest building in the Yonghe Lamasery. It is a three-story pavilion with the roof in *xieshan* style, over 30 meters high, which is linked to the Everlasting Health Pavilion and the Prolonging Appeasement Pavilion on either side by flying galleries. The integrated three pavilions form a magnificent architectural complex.

The Sandalwood Statue of Maitreya

檀香木弥勒佛 in the Pavilion of Ten Thousand Happiness is 26 meters high (18 meters above ground and eight meters below ground), with a diameter of eight meters. The statue is carved from a single trunk of sandalwood. According to the historical records, in the 15th year of the Qianlong reign period (1750), the Tibetan king, who had conflicts with Dalai Lama, tried to arrogate all powers to himself, set up a separatist regime by force of arms, and break away from the Qing government. Meanwhile, the Tibetan king had the official of the Qing government in Tibet and his assistant killed. Upon hearing the news that the Tibetan king had risen in rebellion, the Qing government sent armies to Tibet to aid and console Tibetan officials, further strengthen the Qing government's administration over Tibet, and raise the political status of Dalai Lama. After that Tibet adopted the policy of

integration of religion and politics. To express his gratitude to the Qing government, the Seventh Dalai Lama sent an envoy to the capital to present tributes to the emperor. At that time, Emperor Qianlong, who was preparing for the construction of the Hall of Ten Thousand Happiness, needed large timbers badly. The Seventh Dalai Lama sent people to look for huge trees everywhere, and finally found this large white sandalwood. It took three years for Dalai Lama to transport the white sandalwood to Beijing, and took another three years for artisans to finish carving the trunk of white sandalwood into a Buddhist statue, with the help of Tulku Chahang. Legend has it that over 1,800 meters of yellow satin was used to make a gown for the Buddhist statue. This

❸

❹

well-proportioned, huge and gorgeous Buddha ranks first among all the statues carved with a single trunk in China, and in the world as well.

The Imperial Tablet Pavilion 御碑亭 stands behind the Heavenly King Hall. Constructed in the Qianlong reign period (1736-1795) of the Qing Dynasty, the square pillar-type tablet is about six meters high, making people feel it is extremely high. The inscription on the tablet is written in the Manchu (southern side), Chinese (northern side), Mongolian (eastern side) and Tibetan (western side) languages, hence another name the Stele Pavilion with a Four-language Inscription. The inscription records the origin and evolution of Lamaism, the meaning of "lama," and Emperor Qianlong's attitude toward Lamaism. The Chinese on the northern side shows the handwriting of Emperor Qianlong. The inscription specifies the system of "drawing lots from the golden urn" to determine a "reincarnated boy." In this way the central court had the power to confer a title on and approve a great lama.

---

① The bronze statue of Master Tsongkhapa in the Hall of Wheel of the Law
② A sandalwood statue of Maitreya
③ Pavilion of Ten Thousand Happiness
④ Imperial Tablet Pavilion

*   *   *   *   *   *   *   *

Po Lin Monastery and Tian Tan Buddha (New China: 1949-Present) – the Largest Bronze Buddha in the World

宝莲寺与天坛大佛（新中国：1949 至今）——世界上最大的青铜大佛

The Po Lin Monastery 宝莲寺, also known as the Po Lin Buddhist Temple, is in Ngong Ping Valley on Lantau Island in southwest Hong Kong. Constructed at the end of the 19th century, it ranks first of all the temples in Hong Kong, and enjoys the reputation of being the "South Buddha Kingdom." The famous Giant Buddha sits on Muk Yu Hill in front of the Po Lin Monastery. It is the largest outdoor bronze statue of seated Sakyamuni, showing a wonder of bronze statue casting techniques of modern China.

Tian Tan Buddha 天坛大佛, also known as Giant Buddha, sits at the top of Muk Yu Hill on Lantau Island. There are 260 stone steps from the foot of Muk Yu Hill to the throne of the Giant Buddha. The Buddha's throne is modeled on the Circular Mound Altar in the

Lin Monastery. The Tian Tan Buddha faces south. His right hand is raised, and five fingers stretch out, representing the removal of affliction. His left hand lies on his knee; his palm turns outward; and his fingers point down, signifying human happiness, great power, great mercy and great pity. The Giant Buddha looks serene, dignified and kind, showing the quintessence of sculpture art of the Buddhist statues in the Yungang and Longmen grottoes and the Tang Dynasty.

The bottom of the Giant Buddha has three stories, where the Hall of Merits and Virtues, Exhibition Hall and Memorial Hall are located. A stone stele at the Hall of Merits and Virtues is inscribed the names of the donators.

Temple of Heaven in Beijing, hence the name. The construction started in May 1986 and completed on October 13, 1989. The Buddhist statue is 34 meters high, including 23 meters for the statue and 11 meters for the Lotus Throne. The Giant Buddha is composed of 202 pieces of bronze, weighing 250 tons. On December 29, 1993 (the 17th day of the 11th lunar month), the birthday of Amitabha, a solemn inauguration ceremony for the Tian Tan Buddha was held at the Po

Chinese Bud-dhist Pagodas

中国佛塔概述

The pagoda, commonly known as the Buddhist pagoda, originated from India. Legend has it that after Sakyamuni's nirvana, his disciples cremated his remains, finding a number of "colorful and crystal-clear pearls that cannot be smashed," called relics of the Buddha in Sanskrit. The bodily relics of a Buddha are regarded as deity materials with immeasurable power. According to the instruction by Sakyamuni, founder of Buddhism, his disciples built a pagoda and buried the relics under a pagoda. It was the origin of the Buddhist pagoda. With the passage of time, the pagodas were also used to bury the ashes of things of deceased eminent monks and enshrine Buddhist statues or scriptures.

The Chinese pagodas mainly fall into the following types according to the shapes: One-story pagodas, multi-eave pagodas, pavilion-shaped pagodas, pagodas with the diamond throne, pagodas of Dai ethnic group, and pagoda groups; and in terms of the building materials, they can be divided into stone pagodas, brick pagodas, metal pagodas, wooden pagodas and glazed pagodas. Some pagodas are used to bury gold, silver, corals, pearls and other Buddhist treasures; hence they are also called treasure pagodas.

Now China contains over 3,000 ancient pagodas, each showing its own unique style. The pagodas in north China are imposing and solid; and those in south China are exquisite and beautiful, both showing the high artistic level of Chinese ancient pagodas.

Songyue Temple Pagoda (Northern Wei: 386-534) – the Earliest Pagoda in China

Located in the Songyue Temple, about five kilometers north of Dengfeng City, Henan Province in central China, the Songyue Temple Pagoda was first constructed in the first year of the Zhengguang reign period (520) of the Northern Wei Dynasty, and is the oldest brick pagoda in China. This 12-angle pagoda is over 40 meters high and has 15 stories, a spiral stone round pillar with carvings standing at the top, about two meters high. The body of the pagoda is in the shape of a parabola, and the layer-upon-layer of eaves make it look very beautiful. On each side of the first story of the pagoda is carved the images of Ashoka, king of the Maurya Kingdom of north India, the only example with such an image among all the ancient pagodas in China. Legend has it that there used to be a wooden staircase in the temple, and unfortunately it was later burnt down. Though built with black bricks and yellow earth, this pagoda stands erect and remains intact after 1,500 years, a wonder in the Chinese architectural history.

Famen Temple Pagoda (Tang: 618-907) – a Pagoda Which Holds the Finger Bones of Sakyamuni

法门寺塔（唐代：618—907）——埋藏释迦牟尼佛指的宝塔

Located in Famen Town, about 120 kilometers west of Xi'an City, Shaanxi Province, in northwest China. The exact year for the construction of the temple remains unknown, but it existed as early as in the Eastern Han Dynasty (25-220), with a history of over 1,700 years at least. Originally, it was named King Ashoka Temple. Here Ashoka means "care-free" in Sanskrit, and king refers to the king of ancient Hindu Kingdom (Indian). It was named Famen Temple in the Tang Dynasty, which has been continually used until today.

Legend has it that Ashoka, king of the Hingdu Kingdom, believed in Buddhism. After his death, the monks all over the world built 84,000 pagodas to bury the bodily relics

Chinese Buddhist Pagodas

of Sakyamuni, including 19 such pagodas in China. The Famen Temple Pagoda is one of them. The four-story square wooden pagoda was first constructed in the Zhenguan reign period (627-649) of the Tang Dynasty, and was renamed the Buddha's True Body Pagoda for Protecting the Country in the third year of the Dali reign period (768), which held the finger bones received by the envoys of Emperor Xianzong of the Tang Dynasty. In the Tang Dynasty, all the Chinese people, ranging from the emperor and officials to ordinary folks, were crazy for Buddhism, and seven emperors of the Tang Dynasty held seven grand ceremonies to welcome the finger bones of Buddha. Legend goes that the finger bones of Buddha showed supernatural power once every 30 years, and in the very year, the country would have a bumper harvest and the people would be safe and sound. Then the emperor sent his officials to welcome the Buddha's bones to Chang'an and enshrined them in the palace for three days. After Buddha's bones were transferred to the Famen Temple, it became most famous in the country then.

In the autumn of 1982, heavy rain was pouring down for many days in succession; the foundation of the Famen Temple Pagoda subsided; and half of the pagoda collapsed. In early April 1987, the reconstruction of the pagoda started. When the foundation was being cleaned, an underground palace of the Tang Dynasty was found, from which four finger bones of Buddha (one holy finger bone, and three reproductions of Buddha's finger bones), 121 Buddhist gold and silver vessels, 16 porcelain wares, 17 glass wares, 12 stone objects, 19 lacquer and other objects, over 400 pearls, jade and precious stones and a great amount of silk were excavated. The excavation of a large number of high-quality and well-preserved cultural relics from the Famen Temple was an unprecedented marvel, so that it caused a sensation in the domestic and foreign Buddhist communities. The newly built Famen Temple Museum, and the renovated temple, pagoda and underground palace were open to the public in November 1994.

Kaiyuan Temple Pagoda (Northern Song: 960-1127) – the Highest Pagoda in China

开元寺塔(北宋：960-1127)——中国最高的塔

The Kaiyuan Temple is situated in Dingzhou City, Hebei Province in north China. According to historical accounts, in the Northern Song Dynasty, an eminent monk Hui Neng went on a pilgrimage to Hindu (India) for Buddhist scriptures, and came back with some relics of the Buddha. In the fourth year of the Xianping reign period (1001) of the Northern Song Dynasty, Emperor Zhenzong

issued an edict for the construction of a pagoda. It took 55 years to complete the pagoda on the second year of the Zhihe reign period (1055). An old saying goes "cutting down all the trees in Jiashan Mountain to build Dingzhou Pagoda," proving that the construction of the pagoda was such a great project. In the Song Dynasty, Dingzhou was in the forward position of strategic importance. To ward off Qidan, an ethnic minority in northeast China, the garrison troops used the pagoda to watch the enemy's activities, hence another name "Watching the Enemy Pagoda."

The 11-storey octagonal pagoda sits on a high terrace, 83.7 meters high. It is the tallest of all extant ancient pagodas in the country. The stories are well proportioned, giving the white pagoda a lofty and elegant appearance. Doors were installed on four sides of each story, and each of the two top stories has eight folding doors. At the top of each folding door is decorated with pointed flames, symbolizing the universal enlightenment of the light of Buddha and the smoke curling up from incenses and candles. The pagoda's steeple is composed of subbase decorated with large honeysuckle leaves, an inverted-bowl-shaped top, an iron disc and a pair of bronze beads. The pagoda is divided into the interior and exterior levels, between which is a covered corridor. Inside the pagoda, a winding staircase in the middle leads to the upper stories.

With a history of 1,000 years, the pagoda still stands erect and has not been tilted. After the two serious earthquakes in 1720 and 1884, respectively, the pagoda was partly destroyed. Since the founding of New China, the pagoda has been renovated time and again, making the ancient pagoda well preserved. It is a wonder among all the Chinese ancient pagodas.

✻   ✻   ✻   ✻   ✻   ✻   ✻   ✻

Wooden Pagoda in Yingxian County (Liao: 907-1125) – the Unique Wooden Pagoda in the World

应县木塔(辽代：907-1125)——世界独一无二的木塔

Located in Yingxian County, Shanxi Province in central China, it was built completely with timbers, hence the name. The Wooden Pagoda was first constructed in the second year of the Qingning reign period (1056) of the Liao Dynasty. The Liao was a feudal dynasty set up by Qidan ethnic group in north China from the 10th to the 11th century. To consolidate its rule, the Liao rulers advocated Buddhism and went in for large-scale construction of Buddhist temples and pagodas in Shanxi and Hebei, including the Wooden Pagoda in Yingxian County. The pagoda holds many Buddhist statues and numerous murals of the Liao Dynasty, featuring bright colors and vivid appearances, which are China's artistic treasures. In ancient China, it was the place where the rulers of the past dynasties worshipped Buddha, as well as

the Lookout Tower for commanding and observing wars.

The octagonal Wooden Pagoda in Yingxian County is 67.13 meters high, and the diameter of the first story is 30.27 meters. The exterior of the pagoda is divided into five stories, but there are actually nine stories in the interior, including four built-in stories. According to estimation, the construction of the pagoda used more than 3,500 cubic meters of timber, weighing about 3,000 tons. The Wooden Pagoda has withstood weather erosion, and many wars and strong earthquakes for 950 years, but it stands towering like a giant, with a slight leaning. It is a model of the Chinese ancient wooden structures, a great wonder in the Chinese architecture history, and a unique example in the world.

* * * * * * * *

The 108 Dagobas (Yuan: 1206-1368) – Are They Buddhist Dagobas, or Tomb Pagodas?

一百零八塔(元代：1206—1368)——是佛塔，还是墓塔，谁能说清

On a slope on the western bank of the Yellow River in Qingtongxia City in the Ningxia Hui Autonomous Region in northwest China stand 108 dagobas. We are in no position to find out the exact construction year, but the history books published in the mid Ming Dynasty called them ancient dagobas. As they are in the similar shape of the White Dagoba in Miaoying Temple in Beijing built in the Yuan Dynasty (1206-1368), archaeologists believe they were built in the Yuan Dynasty.

There are 108 dagobas in total, arranged in twelve rows, tapering all the odd numbers from one to nineteen, in the shape of a large equilateral triangle. The largest solid dagoba at the top of the triangle is in the shape of an inverted bowl. Pure white in color and built with bricks, it sits on an octagonal sumeru throne and has a pearl-shaped top. Other dagobas have the basically same shape, but they are smaller.

Chinese Buddhist Pagodas

Why were 108 dagobas built? There are many explanations. One saying goes: Buddhism believes every human being has 108 worries in the life. To help people get rid of all the worries, ancestors built 108 Buddhist dagobas here. The number 108 is the common Buddhist number. A devout Buddhist is to wear a rosary with 108 beads, say prayers 108 times in acknowledgement of man's sins and toll the bell for 108 times to stave off such unlucky occurrences. Another saying goes: In ancient times, it was a strategic point where 108 generals laid down their lives. To commemorate the heroes, 108 dagobas were built.

After the founding of New China, the dagoba complex has been repaired and renovated. Now the 108 dagobas have become one of the famous tourist attractions in Ningxia, together with the Yellow River and the Qingtong Gorge Key Water Control Project.

Diamond Throne Pagoda in Zhenjue Temple (Ming: 1364-1644) – a Pagoda That Survived a Raging Fire

真觉寺金刚宝座塔(明代：1364—1644)——在烈火中永生的金刚塔

Commonly known as the Five Pagoda Temple, the Zhenjue Temple is close to Baishiqiao in Haidian District, Beijing. The temple was first constructed in the Yongle reign period (1403-1424) of the Ming Dynasty. Legend has it that once an eminent monk of India came from the Western Regions, and presented five gold Buddhist

statues and a model of the Diamond Throne Pagoda to the Emperor Chengzu of the Ming Dynasty as gifts. The emperor met the eminent monk at the Hall of Military Prowess in the former Imperial Palace, and discussed scriptures with him. They had a most agreeable chat. The emperor named him National Master, gave him a gold seal as a gift, and issued an order for building this imperial temple. In the ninth year of the Chenghua reign period (1473) of the Ming Dynasty, a stone pagoda was set up according to the model of the Diamond Throne Pagoda presented by the Indian monk. In the late Qing Dynasty, the temple was burnt down, but the Diamond Throne Pagoda built with bricks inside and stone outside survived.

On the four sides of the foundation of the Diamond Throne Pagoda are carved five kinds of animals, i.e., lions, horses, elephants, peacocks and sheep, as well as footprints of Buddhas, relief sculptures of Buddhist symbols, floral designs, Sanskrit letters and

Tibetan scripts. Five small pagodas rise from the base of the Diamond Throne Pagoda, representing Buddhas of the east, west, south, north and central. It is the oldest one among all such extant pagodas in China. The pagoda is 17 meters high, with a stone staircase leading to the top. Five small stone pagodas and one square pavilion with a glass cover stand at the top of the pagoda. The whole pagoda, including the foundation, is covered with Buddhist statues, Sanskrit letters and religious patterns. Though in the similar shape of the Indian architecture, the pagoda shows the traditional ethnic style in the structure and carving techniques. It is a wonder in the China-India cultural exchange history.

In 1987, the Beijing Art Museum of Stone Carvings was founded in the temple, with the Diamond Throne Pagoda as the mainstay. As the first comprehensive museum of stone carvings in the open air, it introduces the development and colorful features of the Chinese stone carving art.

⁂ ⁂ ⁂ ⁂ ⁂ ⁂ ⁂ ⁂

Pelkor Chode Monastery Pagoda (Ming:1364-1644) – a Riddle of a Group of Chinese Pagodas

白居寺塔(明代：1364–1644)——中国塔群之谜

Lying at the foot of Zongshan Mountain in Gyangze County, over 100 kilometers east of

Xigaze in Tibet in southwest China, the Pelkor Chode Monastery Pagoda is more than 3,900

meters above sea level. The construction of the pagoda started in the second year of the Xuande reign period of Emperor Xuanzong (1427) of the Ming Dynasty, and was not completed 10 years later. The Pelkor Chode Monastery was built under the situation that all the sects in Tibet sat as equals at the same table with each other, so all the sects, such as Sakya, Gelug and Buton, could coexist peacefully with each other in the temple. As each Buddhist sect in Tibet holds five to six dratsang (halls) in the temple, the Pelkor Chode Monastery has a special position and influence in the Tibetan Buddhism history.

The Pelkor Chode Monastery consists of two parts: the temple and Pelkor Chorten (or Multi-door Pagoda), which is composed of the base, pagoda body and top. The exterior of the pagoda is divided into nine stories, but there are actually 13 stories in the interior, with a total of 146 angles. The pagoda is 42 meters high; the stories are linked by timbers and stones; and the upper story is smaller than the below one, shrinking story by story and showing a very special architectural style. Each of the first to the fifth stories has four sides and eight angles; and the sixth to the ninth stories are round in shape. The pagoda has 108 doors, 77 Buddhist halls, niches and sutra halls, hence it enjoys a reputation of being the "Temple in a Pagoda." On the door of the pagoda are many beautiful relief sculptures, such as flying dragons, running lions and walking elephants. The hall houses 10,000 statues of Buddha of Infinity, hence another name the "Ten-Thousand-Buddha Pagoda."

The Pelkor Chode Monastery that has absorbed the religious architectural characteristics of Myanmar, Nepal, India and the Chinese inland shows its own unique style. It is an only Buddhist pagoda of such kind in the Chinese architecture history.

Emin Pagoda (Qing: 1644-1911) – a Wonder of Islamic Architecture Art

额敏塔(清代：1644–1911)——伊斯兰教建筑艺术的奇迹

Located in the suburbs of Turpan City, Xinjiang in northwest China, the Emin Pagoda is also known as Emin Bao'en Pagoda, and Lord Su Pagoda, which was constructed in the 42nd year of the Qianlong reign period (1777) of the Qing Dynasty. Legend has it that it was built by Su Laiman, prefect of Turpan, to commemorate the merits and achievements of his father, Emin Hezhuo. But the recent research proves that it was built by Emin

Hezhuo himself before his death. The cylinder pagoda, 44 meters high, is built with earth and bricks, and decorated with the rhombus, mountain, wave, petal and other patterns. The pagoda has neither a foundation stone, nor a timber, with only a spiral pillar built with bricks in the center supporting the whole pagoda. It is a famous artistic architectural structure of Islam, and a wonder of Chinese ancient pagodas.

Yunyan Pagoda (Republic of China: 1919-1949) – the Largest Mother-and-Son Pagoda in China

允燕塔(民国：1919—1949)——中国最大的母子塔

Standing in Yunyan Mountain, 15 kilometers southeast of the seat of Yingjiang County, Yunnan Province in southwest China, the Yunyan Pagoda was first built in the Republic of China, and was renovated in 1956. It consists of a main pagoda in the center and 44 small pagodas in the surrounding areas. The main pagoda is about 20 meters high and sits on a square throne, which is 19.5 meters long and has a five-story altar. On each side of every story stand seven pagodas, and on each of the four corners from the second to the fifth story stands a pagoda. The main pagoda decorated with lotus petal and warrior patterns is imposing and magnificent. The body of the pagoda covered with gold leaves is glittering; and some bells hung at the top jingle in the wind. It is the one of the largest Buddhist pagodas of Theravada of Southern Buddhism in South China.

Chinese Grottoes

中国石窟概述

Grottoes are caves of various kinds chiseled according to the physical features of the mountains. Having similar functions with the Buddhist temples, these caves house the sculptures or statues of Buddha and Buddhist figures in the convenience for Buddhist believers to pay their respects to Buddha and carry forward the Buddhist culture.

China boasts many grottoes in all parts but there is no exact figure about them. Rough estimation shows that they are in several hundred.

Everybody knows China has three great famous grottoes. They are the Yungang Grottoes in Datong, Longmen Grottoes in Luoyang and Mogao Grottoes in Dunhuang. Others believe the figure should be four including the Maijishan Grottoes in Tianshui or the Thousand-Buddha Cave in Kizil.

The building of grottoes began during the second and third centuries in China and some lasted for 1,000 years and went through a dozen dynasties. These grottoes are seldom in the world for their large scales, hardwork in construction, the great amounts of intact stone statues, sculptures and murals, and rich contents. Some house only clay statues or colorful murals owing to the loose quality of cliffs. These grottoes provide valuable and rare cultural gems for the entire mankind.

Mogao Grottoes (Pre-Qin-Yuan: 350-1368) with Most Murals in China

莫高窟（前秦 — 元代：350—1368）——中国壁画最多的石窟

❶

Dunhuang was an important town along the ancient Silk Road. Traders and tourists who entered and exited the Yumen Pass and Yangguan Pass always visited the Mogao Grottoes to worship the Buddha here. They needed the Buddha to protect them while Buddhists needed their support for the construction of the grottoes. In this way, the Mogao Grottoes flourished steadily.

The Mogao Grottoes are located 25 kilometers southeast of Dunhuang City, Gansu Province in northwest China. The first cave came under construction in 366 or the second year of the Jianyuan reign of the pre-Qin Dynasty. It is said there was a monk named Le Zun who came to the Singing Sands Mountain from the Central Plains. Suddenly, he saw the mountain glistened, like thousands of Buddhas emerged in golden rays. The monk believed the mountain be a sacred place and chiseled the first cave on the cliffs with the donated money. In it he recited the Buddhist scripture. Later, other monks came for pilgrimage and the second, third and more caves were chiseled around the first one.

The Mogao Grottoes were chiseled on the eastern cliffs of the Singing Sands Mountain. In five rows, the grottoes extend for more than 1,600 meters from south to north. Through weathering and man-made destroy, only 492 cave-temples, more than 45,000 square meters of frescos, 2,415 painted sculptures built during the 10 dynasties from the North Wei Dynasty (386-534) to the Yuan Dynasty (1206-1368) are intact, so as five wood structure buildings with lotus column stands and thousands of floor tiles from the Tang and Song dynasties (618-1279). The Mogao Grottoes are a comprehensive artistic palace composed of buildings, paintings and sculptures. Originally, there were halls outside the caves

❷

3

and historical figures are delicate in design and lovely. If all the frescos put into a two-meter-high picture roll, it will extend for 25 kilometers long. The Mogao Grottoes are the largest grotto art treasure with richest contents in China.

Buddhist Scriptures Cave 藏经洞, or No. 17 Cave of the Mogao Grottoes in Dunhuang, was built during the late Tang Dynasty (836-907) in the memory of senior monk Hong Bian of Hexi from the late Tang Dynasty. Chiseled on the wall along the path to No. 16 Cave, it is one meter above the ground, 2.5-2.7 meters long and wide and three meters high. With a double corbel bracket ceiling, the cave has a space of 19 cubic meters. On its northern wall there is a fresco of two Bodhidruma trees with their leaves and branches growing together. Hanging from the tree on the east is a bottle filled with pure water and standing by it is Bhiksuni with a round fan in his hands. Hanging from the tree on the west is a bag and standing by it is a girl wearing man's clothes. Beneath the trees is a rectangular terrace with a sitting statue of Monk Hong Bian on it. This cave

which were connected by plank roads or wooden corridors. The largest cave is some 40 meters high, 30 meters long and wide while the smallest is only 30 centimeters high. All clay statues are painted and stand single or in groups. The Buddha stands in the middle and is flanked by his disciplines, Bodhisattva, Heavenly King or guardians, three at minimum and 11 at maximum, with the largest being 33 meters and the smallest being 10 centimeters high only. Their characteristics and expressions are exaggerated in heavy colors. Frescos have different themes. Some display Buddha, the history of Buddhism and the stories of Buddhism while others tell fairy tales and the donators. All the frescos including the oldest 40-square-meter-large *Map of Wutai Mountains, Picture of Travel by Zhang Yichao and His Wife* and others of flowers, trees, gods

4

was sealed before its completion, before the monks' fleeing from the war launched by Western Xia people to overcome Dunhuang in the early 11th century. The monks did not return again and the cave was sealed for 900 years before it was found while cleaning the path to No. 16 Cave in 1900 or the 26th year of the Guangxu reign of the Qing Dynasty. Then a total of 50,000 pieces of cultural relics including sutras, books, embroidery and paintings were discovered. One-sixth of the books are written in various minority languages such as Tibetan, ancient Uygur language, ancient Indian and ancient Sogd languages. Also found were several hundred pieces of paintings on silk and embroideries. Except Buddhist scriptures, books on Taoism and Confucian classics,

there were historical books, books of poems, story books, folk literary books, books on local historical records, household registrations, account books, chronic events, receipts, letters and others, including books on cultural relics from the Jin Dynasty to the Song Dynasty, some 10 dynasties from the 4th to the 11th centuries. The discovery has aroused great concern of the experts at home and abroad. Since then more and more people have paid great attention to the study of Dunhuang documents, literature and art, and cultural relics and a special research branch of Dunhuang art has been developed.

Nine-Story Building 九层楼, or No. 96 Cave of the Mogao Grottoes in Dunhuang, got its name for its nine rows of eaves. It houses a 33-meter-high painted clay statue of

sitting Maitreya. Outside the cave there are two passages for people to see the face and waist of the Buddha closely and for light shed on the head and waist of the statue. The building is as tall as the cliff and sits in the half way of the cliff. This magnificent building is one of the famous spots of the Mogao Grottoes.

After the Buddhist Scriptures Cave was found in 1900, the historical and cultural relics inside the cave were damaged seriously by the imperialists and great amounts of valuable cultural relics were stolen. After the Dunhuang Art Research Institute was established in 1943, many cultural relics had been repaired, maintained and studied. After the national liberation in 1949, the institute was renamed as the Dunhuang Cultural Relics Re-

search Institute and an overall maintenance of all the caves in Dunhuang was carried out. In 1984 the Dunhuang Research Institute was established. In the past few decades, the scholars at home and abroad who have great interest in Dunhuang art have formed a special academic branch for studying the Dunhuang art. The Mogao Grottoes in Dunhuang have been included into the World Heritage List by the UNESCO.

---

① Mogao Grottoes
② The Nine-Story Building in Mogao Grottoes
③ A color statue of the Tang Dynasty in Mogao Grottoes
④ The documents of the Tang Dynasty in Buddhist Scriptures Cave
⑤ A color mural in Mogao Grottoes
⑥ Overlooking Mogao Grottoes

✳   ✳   ✳   ✳   ✳   ✳   ✳   ✳

Maijishan Grottoes (Late Qin-Qing: 384-1911) – the Largest Museum of Sculptures in the East

麦积山石窟(后秦－清代：384—1911)——被称为 "东方最大的雕塑馆"

In northwest China, the Maijishan Grottoes are more than 30 kilometers southeast of Tianshui City, Gansu Province. The grottoes are more than 150 meters high and got its name because it is like a pile of wheat straws. The Maijishan Grottoes are one of the four

famous grottoes in China.

Historical records show that the Maijishan Grottoes were first built during the late Qin Dynasty (384-417) while a Buddhist temple was being built. Through 1,500 years of more than 10 dynasties from the Northern Wei (386-

534) to the Qing (1644-1911), the grottoes were repaired and expanded constantly. Today there are 194 caves intact which house some 7,200 clay or stone statues (including 1,000 ones being one meter tall or taller) and more than 1,300 square meters of frescos. The Maijishan Grottoes are one of the most famous ones in China. The caves were chiseled on the 70-80-meter-high cliffs, some 20-30 meters from the mountain base. The caves stand one above another, like wax cells in honey combs. In 734 or the 22nd year of the Kaiyuan reign of the Tang Dynasty, a strong earthquake happened in Tianshui split the Maiji Mountain into eastern and western cliffs

which have been linked through a plank path today. Now there are 54 caves on the eastern cliff and 140 caves on the western cliff.

Famous as the "largest museum of sculp-

tures in the east," the Maijishan Grottoes house thousands of life-like round sculptures such as the statues of solemn Buddha, kings, Bodhisattva and disciples. Some smile, some speak in each other's ears, while others are in the images of lovely and wise girls and boys. The tallest statue of Amitalha is 16 meters high and the shortest is only 10 centimeters high. All sculptures from the statue of Buddha to the statue of an ox with golden horns and silver hoofs by the foot of the Heavenly King are all vivid and demonstrate a delicate craftsmanship. They are personified and kind but not mysterious.

The Maiji Mountain is a fantastic peak and it is warm in the winter and cold in the summer. In the autumn, it drizzles frequently and the mountain is covered by clouds. Climbing up the 70-odd-meter-high Seven-Buddha Hall (or Flower-Spreading Building) you spread the flowers which will rise up and up following the up-flowing air. Also in autumn, the green sea composed of pine trees and the ridges and peaks turn the mountain into one of the famous tourist spot in China.

✻   ✻   ✻   ✻   ✻   ✻   ✻   ✻

Yungang Grottoes (Northern Wei: 386-534) – Museum of the Earliest Stone Carvings in China

云冈石窟（北魏：386—534）——中国最早的石雕艺术馆

In north China, the Yungang Grottoes are   16 kilometers west of Datong City in Shanxi

Province, at the southern foot of the Wuzhou Mountain. It is named after the highest place of the mountain. The grottoes were chiseled according to the geographic conditions of the mountain and extend for one kilometer from east to west. The 51,000 stone statues in the 53 caves make the Yungang Grottoes one of the largest grotto groups in China and one of the world-known treasure houses of art.

The Yungang Grottoes were first hewn in 460 or the first year of the Heping reign of the Northern Wei Dynasty. Most of the principal caves had been completed by the year 494 or the 18th year of the Taihe reign, when the Northern Wei Dynasty moved its capital to Luoyang in Henan Province. The whole carving work lasted for more than 60 years, extending into the Zhengguang reign (520-525), and involved some 40,000 people. Even the Buddhists from the present-day Sri Lanks joined the artistic creation of the Yungang

Grottoes. Later these caves were repaired on several occasions and a Buddhist temple was added, including two large-scale repairs during the Liao and Jin dynasties (907-1234).

The Wuhua Caves 五华洞 are located in the middle section of the Yungang Grottoes and are composed of five caves of Nos. 9-13. They became famous because the statues were colored during the Qing Dynasty (1644-1911). On the ceiling are carved with female dancers and singers holding vertical bamboo flutes, pipa (four-stringed lute), harps, flutes or drums. They provide important materials for the study of the history of the Chinese music instruments.

The Tanyao Five Caves 昙曜五窟 are located in the middle section of the Yungang Grottoes and composed of caves of Nos. 16-20. They are the five earliest caves hewn under the supervision of Monk Tanyao in the reign years of Emperor Wencheng of the

Northern Wei Dynasty (384-534). So they got the name. The principal statue of Buddha is more than 13 meters high. It is said the statue was hewn after the fifth emperor of the Northern Wei Dynasty.

The Outdoor Buddha 露天大佛 is located at the western end of the middle section or No. 20 Cave. The main statue is a sitting Sakyamuni which is 13.7 meters high. Carved from a strong rock, the statue is intact and is a representative of the statues in the Yungang Grottoes.

Among the three largest grottoes in China, the Yungang Grottoes is famous for their magnificent and colorful stone sculptures and rich contents. Until today, they still demonstrate strong artistic charming. The tallest statue of Buddha is 17 meters high while the smallest being only several centimeters. Bodhisattva, guardians and Apsaras and other images are vivid. The carvings of dragons, lions, tigers, birds with golden wings and other kinds of animals as well luxuriant plants demonstrate excellent craftsmanship and development from the artistic traditions of the Qin and Han dynasties (221 B.C.- A.D. 220) and absorbed those from abroad. They occupy important positions in the history of Chinese arts. Today they have been included into the World Heritage List by the UNESCO.

Chinese Grottoes

Longmen Grottoes (Northern Wei-Tang: 386-907) with Most Statues in China

Located in central China, the Longmen Grottoes are on the banks of the Yihe River, 13 kilometers south of Luoyang City in Henan Province and one of the three largest grottoes in China. Also they are one of the world-known treasure houses of art. Two hills stand on the both banks of the Yihe River, like a natural watchtower and is a scenic spot with hills and waters. In ancient times, the kings and emperors from various historical periods came here to pay their respects to Buddha. Later they were renamed the Longmen Grottoes.

The construction of the Longmen Grottoes began around 493 or the 17th year of the Taihe reign after Emperor Xiaowen of the Northern Wei Dynasty moved his capital to Luoyang.

The construction lasted for 400 years from the Eastern and Western Wei dynasties (534-556) to the Tang Dynasty (618-907). The niches on both hills are like wax cells in honey combs. The representative caves include the Guyang Cave, Binyang Cave Group, Lotus Cave, Medical Inscription Cave hewn during the Northern Wei Dynasty (386-534), and Qianxi Temple, Ten-Thousand-Buddha Cave, Ancestor-Worshipping Temple, and Buddhist Scriptures-Reading Temple built during the Tang Dynasty (618-907). In total there are more than 2,100 niches, 97,300 statues of Buddha, more than 3,600 inscriptions and tablets, and 39 Buddhist towers. This group of artistic statues provides rich and important materials for the study of Chinese ancient his-

tory and art. Apsaras in these caves fly amid clouds, dance with fruits in their hands, play music instruments and sing songs, or spread rain drops and flowers. In light and elegant postures, they are charming. The inscriptions and tablets such as the famous "20 Excellent Works of Longmen" and the "Inscriptions on Watchtower to Niches" written by famous calligrapher Zhu Suiliang from the Tang Dynasty are valuable pieces of the Chinese calligraphic works.

Guyang Cave 古阳洞 in the southern section of the Western Hill was built in 493 when Emperor Xiaowen moved the capital of the Northern Wei Dynasty to Luoyang. The cave was one of the earliest with rich cultural

contents. On two side walls inside the cave carved three rows of niches. The statue of Buddha with glory behind is magnificent and splendid. The patterns and decorative lines are rich and colorful. The statues of the supporters look solemn and honest, vivid and dynamic. The cave is full of sculptures and carvings and houses 19 of the "20 Excellent Works of Longmen," providing rare cultural relics for studying calligraphic history in China.

Binyang Cave Group 宾阳洞 in the northern section of the Western Hill is composed of three caves: Southern Cave, Central Cave and Northern Cave. The chiseling of the Central Cave began in 500 or the first year of

the Jingming reign and completed in 523 or the fourth year of the Zhengguang reign of the Northern Wei Dynasty. The construction of the cave lasted for 24 years and involved more than 800,000 workdays. The statues of Sakyamuni and his disciples have pretty faces and their clothes have regular folders and more wrinkles, demonstrating the special features of the carvings of the Northern Wei Dynasty. The ceiling is a lotus precious canopy painted 10 female dancers and singers as well as supporters. The inside walls by the entrance are once decorated with bas-relief carvings in four rows of "Story of Vimalakirti," "Story of Life of Buddha," "Emperor Worshipping Buddha," "Empress worshipping Buddha," and "Images of 10 Gods." Of them, the pictures of "Emperor Worshipping Buddha" and "Empress Worshipping Buddha" were stolen abroad in the old days.

Medical Prescription Cave 药方洞 in the northern section of the Western Hill was first hewn in the late Northern Wei Dynasty (386-534) and completed in the Tang period ruled by Wu Zetian. The construction lasted for 200 years. On the both sides of its entrance are more than 140 prescriptions for curing 37 kinds of common diseases chiseled in the Northern Qi Dynasty (550-577). They are the oldest stone carved prescriptions discovered in China and the oldest form to publicize medical sciences in the world. The statues of

Buddha and their disciples inside the cave and the warriors outside, were chiseled in the Northern Qi Dynasty.

Ancestor-Worshipping Temple 奉先寺 at the southern end of the Western Hill was first hewn in the early reign years of Tang Emperor Gaozong and completed in 675 or the second year of the Shangyuan reign of the Tang Dynasty. This temple is the largest outdoor niche of the Longmen Grottoes and is a representative of the sculptures of the Tang Dynasty. The niche is 42 meters from east to west and 36 meters from south to north. The main statue of Vairocana is 17.14 meters high, the tallest statue of Buddha among the

Longmen Grottoes. The records on its construction show that Wu Zetian donated 20,000 strings out of her cosmetic money for the construction of this temple and together with her ministers joined the ceremony held on an auspicious day to unveil a newly finished statue of Vairocana.

The morning is the best time to visit the Longmen Grottoes, with the sunlight shed directly on the Western Hill and good for taking photos. Today the Longmen Grottoes have been included into the World Heritage List by the UNESCO.

Leshan Great Buddha (Tang: 618-907) – the Tallest Stone Buddha in the World

In southwest China, Leshan Great Buddha is standing on the eastern bank of the East Minjiang River in Leshan City, Sichuan Province, at the confluence of the Minjiang, Qingyi and Dadu rivers. The Great Buddha was first chiseled by Monk Haitong in 713, the first year of the Kaiyuan reign of the Tang Dynasty and was completed in 803 or the 19th year of the Zhengyuan reign under the supervision of the Military Commissioner Wei Gao.

The construction lasted for 90 years. This seated Buddha stands against the mountain and faces the river, with his head as tall as the mountain. It measures 71 meters from top to bottom, has a head 14.7 meters long and 10 meters wide, ears 7 meters long, eyes 3.3 meters wide, and shoulder 24 meters wide. His ears are big enough for two persons standing inside. Each of the 10.92-meter-long feet can accommodate some 100 persons to sit on.

On the cliff behind the Buddha statue, to the left, stands the Haishi Cave. In it Monk Haitong once lived when the statue was being chiseled. But unfortunately, he died before the statue was completed.

The Great Buddha was repaired in January 2002. A terrace at its foot was expanded to have a floor space of 150 square meters. At the same time, its lotus flower shape was restored. Thus the terrace can keep the statue away from the erosion by the river water and also provide more space for tourists to pass through.

To the right of the statue, a nine-bend plank path has been built. Going down the cliff through the path, tourists can have an upward look of the statue. "There is a statue of Buddha on the mountain and the statue of Buddha looks like a mountain." The Great Buddha is elegant and magnificent and is the tallest stone statue of Buddha in China or even in the world. Today it has been included into the World Heritage List by the UNESCO.

Stone Carvings in Dazu County (Tang and Song: 618-1279) – a Story About Buddhism Easily Understood by Ordinary People

大足石刻（唐宋时期：618–1279）——老百姓一看就懂的佛教故事

In southwest China, stone carvings are in Dazu County, 160 kilometers west of Chongqing. They were first created in 892 or the first year of the Jingfu reign of the Tang Dynasty and completed in the late Southern Song Dynasty (1127-1279). Some 40 groups of more than 50,000 pieces of stone carvings on Confucianism, Buddhism and Taoism are scattered within the boundary of the county, especially on North Hill and Precious Crown Hill. Illustrating excellent workmanship, these intact carvings are representative of China's late excellent grotto art and have pushed China's grotto art into a high and new stage.

Stone carvings in Dazu emerged after the grottoes in north China declined. Their contents and techniques of expression demonstrate they are not the continuity or repeat of the images of the previous stage but they rep-resent the features of the time. Talking about the contents, they mainly display the life and death, paradise and hell, being a grateful recipient of royal favors and paying a debt of gratitude, cultivating one's mind and awakening, ascetic practice and attaining Buddhahood through continuous pictures. Thus they have turned China's grotto art of Buddhism realistic. Here we introduce you some stone carvings on the Precious Crown Hill only.

Stone Carvings on the Precious Crown Hill 宝顶山石刻 are 15 kilometers northeast of Dazu County. Here was once a base of Chengdu Yoga branch of Esoteric School of Buddhism with Liu Benzun, a native of Leshan in Sichuan, as its founder. In the late Tang Dynasty, when Esoteric in north China declined, Liu carried out Yoga and founded its branch through his cultivation. Since then Buddhist Esoteric School developed in Sichuan areas.

The stone carvings on the Precious Crown Hill were created by famous monk Zhao Zhifeng from the Southern Song Dynasty. Following Liu's concepts, Zhao publicized Buddhism on the Precious Crown Hill and was praised as the master of the sixth generation. From the sixth year of the Chunxi reign to the ninth year of the Chunyou reign of the Southern Song Dynasty (1179-1249), Zhao traveled a lot for collecting money and sponsored the hewing of ten thousand of statues of Buddha on the cliffs of the Lesser Buddha Bay and Greater Buddha Bay and established an unprecedented ground for publicizing Esoteric branch of Buddhism in China.

3

The stone carvings on the Precious Crown Hill, or the Great Buddha Bay, are on the East, South and North Cliffs. The niche grottoes are as high as the mountain and the statues of Buddha are concentrated on the 2,600-square-meter cliff surfaces being 4-14 meters high. The Great Buddha Bay is in a U shape and the cliffs are 15-30 meters high and 500 meters long. In total, there are some 30 huge carvings and the most famous ones are "The Six-Way Samsara," "Broad Treasure Building," "Images of Three Saints of Hua-yen," "Thousand-Armed Guanyin," "Sakyamuni Entering Nirvana," "Nine Dragons and Prince," "Ming King Sits on a Lotus Platform Supported by a Phoenix," "Grand Service of Vairocana," "Story from the Scripture on the Kindness of Parents," "Amitayur-dhyana Sutra," "Ten Great Vidyarajas" and "Perfect Enlightenment." These images were created by famous monk Zhao Zhifeng with the themes of Buddhist stories. No two images are the same. By each image there is sutra and introductory words about the image. All images are like picture books, quite different with those found in other grottoes.

"The Six-Way Samsara" 六道轮回图 in No.3 Cave symbolizes Buddhist causality, transmigration, twelve links and repayment for both kindness and wickedness. In this carving, a ghost holds a six-interest wheel in his long arms. In the middle of the wheel sits a person and releases out from his heart six rays that means all are from the heart. Six rays divide the wheel into six parts that reflect six repayments: three good ones and three bad ones. Good repayments for good things you do with kind heart and bad repayments for bad things you do with evil heart. With best repayment you can go to heaven while with worst repayment you will go to hell to be eaten by ghosts and become animals.

"Thousand-Armed Guanyin" 千手观音像 is chiseled on an area of 88 square meters of the cliff. The statue of Guanyin is less than three meters in height. Sitting on a lotus, Guanyin wears a crown and has a serious appearance. Her hands are in salutation by putting palms together. In addition it has 1,007 arms spreading on the cliff. On the palm of each arm has an eye and each hand holds a pagoda, a weapon, a tool, a piece of music instrument, a stationery, a piece of gem or a Buddhist treasure. Its arms in different shapes are like a peacock in its pride. This statue is praised as one of the wonders under heaven.

"Sakyamuni Entering Nirvana" 释迦牟尼涅盘像 is mainly composed of a statue of Sakyamuni which is 31 meters long, lying on the right side with right shoulder buried in the ground. A dozen disciples in front of the statue are coming out from the underground with flowers, fruits, cookies, jewelry or clothes in their hands. In the clouds above the statue stand nine goddesses, holding flowers or fruits. The disciples and goddesses are sending assumption of Sakyamuni. Standing in the middle of the goddesses is his mother flanked by his wife and aunt. According to the Buddhism, his mother should bend her knee to him. But Chinese paid attention to the filial piety and Buddhism in the Song Dynasty was influenced by Confucianism. So his mother stands in the clouds to say goodbye to Sakyamuni. In front of the statue there is a nine-bend Yellow River. A legend says the disciples are reluctant to say goodbye to him and then Sakyamuni waves his hand to have a river to stop his disciples.

The stone carvings on the Precious Crown Hill show that when Buddhism was declining in China, Buddhism was combined with Confucianism. The stone carvings on the Precious Crown Hill have themes from reality and the statues are realistic and folk. Except statues of Buddha, there are many statues of persons in the Song-style dresses, with themes from folk life. All these are of important value for understanding and studying the development of Buddhism and Buddhist art in the Song Dynasty. Dazu stone carvings have been included into the World Heritage List by the UNESCO.

---

① "Sakyamuni Entering Nirvana"
② "The Six-way Samsara"
③ Thousand-Armed Guanyin

China's Rural Towns and Villages

中国乡村概述

China is a country composed of many ethnic groups. It has a rural population of 900 million living in 680,000 natural administrative villages. China has varied topographic conditions and vast rural areas with big gaps in temperatures. Different ethnic groups have different customs. In the past these rural areas had poor communications facilities. As a result these closed areas maintained their special and varied architectural styles, which are of the ordinary people in China. Such unique villages and residential houses represent the traditional architecture styles of China.

Rural architectures have rich contents. According to geographic divisions, they fall into following categories: the compound with houses around a courtyard in north China, the loess cave-house in northwest China, the arched house on grassland in Inner Mongolia, the earthen house with a flat roof in northeast China's plains, the wooden or bamboo houses built up above the ground in mountainous areas in southwest China, the earthen houses in hilly areas in Fujian Province, the defensive blockhouses in Kaiping in Guangdong Province, Drum Towers of the Dong ethnic group in Guizhou Province, Danba blockhouses in Tibetan communities in Sichuan Province, the pile dwellings in south Hunan Province, and mushroom-shaped houses of the Hani ethnic group in Yunnan Province. All such rural residential houses are of great historical, cultural and tourist value and are an important component of architectural wonders in China.

Ancient Village of Xidi (Northern Song-Qing: 960-1911) – Museum of Chinese Dwellings

Ancient village of Xidi is eight kilometers east of Yixian County Seat in Anhui Province. It was first built during the Northern Song Dynasty (960-1127) and has a history of more than 900 years. Today the village has 99 lanes and two streets paved with flagstones. The 124 residential houses from the Ming (1368-1644) and Qing (1644-1911) dynasties are famous for their stone carved gate flowers and stone carved windows. Each house has a meticulously carved stone arch of the gateway of different patterns. Every household has one or several courtyards in which are flower beds, water ponds, hollow windows, short walls, and stone and brick carvings, looking delicate, beautiful and

pleasing to both the eye and the mind. Each household has its own well with a stone ring from which the host gets water for making tea for their guests. It is praised as a wonderful thing of the village. The representative houses in the village are the Officialdom Residence, Ruiyu House, Taoli House, Yanggao Hall and Qingyu Hall.

The ancient dwellings in Xidi Village are seldom at home and abroad and the village is praised as the museum of Chinese dwellings. Today the village has become a famous tourist destination and attracts flocks of Chinese and foreign experts to appreciate residential houses there. Today the Xidi Village has been included into the World Heritage List by the UNESCO.

Ancient Town of Zhouzhuang (Yuan: 1206-1368) – a Wonder Found by a Foreigner

周庄古镇(元代：1206—1368)———被外国人发现的一个奇观

In east China, Zhouzhuang is 38 kilometers southeast of Suzhou, Jiangsu Province, or 80 kilometers west of Shanghai. In 1984, the famous painter Chen Yifei created a traditional oil painting entitled "Collections of Hometown" with a twin bridgeas its theme. Later the painting was printed on a first-day cover by the United Nations. Since then Zhouzhuang has been known by the people from other countries.

Zhouzhuang is a 900-odd-year-old town and was established in 1086 or the first year of the Yuanyou reign of the Northern Song Dynasty by Zhou Digong. So it was named Town of Zhouzhuang. In the mid-Yuan Dynasty (1206-1368), Shen You, father of a rich man Shen Wansan in southern Jiangsu, moved here from Nanxun in Huzhou and bought the land. Dealing with trade, Shen family developed gradually and became a town.

Most intact buildings in Zhouzhuang were built during the Ming and Qing dynasties (1368-1911). The two horizontal rivers in the town cross with two vertical ones and the residential houses were built along the riverside streets. Today there are 14 ancient bridges over these rivers. The streets are narrow and zigzagged. The row upon row of ancient buildings, waterside pavilions and stone bridges constitute a beautiful scene of the waterside village in south Jiangsu Province. The main tourist spots include the Zhangs' house, the Shens' house, former residence of Ye Chulun, mini building, Quanfu Temple in Nanhu Garden, Dengxu Taoist Temple, Twin Bridge, Fu'an Bridge and Zhenfeng Bridge. Town of Zhouzhuang is one of famous tourist destinations.

China's Rural Towns and Villages

Ancient Hongcun Village (Ming and Qing:1368-1911) – a Village in the Shape of a Cow Abdomen

宏村古村(明清:1368–1911)——中国有个牛肚子村庄

Situated in central China, Hongcun Village is 11 kilometers north of Yixian County in Anhui Province. This village was built during the Ming and Qing dynasties. It faces south and sits against the Xuegang Mountain and with the Yongxi and Yangzhan rivers in front. The rivers run from north to south and go by the village. A stream goes through the village, like a cow bowel having nine bends and 18 turnings. It passes through the Yuetang Pond (like a cow abdomen) in the middle of the village before emptying into a lake in the southern part of the village. The whole village looks like a lying buffalo. With an original conception, it is a wonder in history of Chinese and foreign architectures.

The crescent-shaped Nanhu Lake in the southern part of the village is like a mirror which reflects the mountains around. On the bank stands the Nanhu Academy of Classical Learning, a place for studying knowledge. Today the village boasts one house from the Ming Dynasty and 132 houses from the Qing Dynasty. All the houses have a screen wall

behind the main entrance, stone carved arch over the gateway and wooden door leaves each. Behind the main entrance there is a hall with painted ceiling. The house demonstrates elegant decorations and delicate carvings. The most typical ones are Chengzhi Hall and Jingxiu Hall built by the salt businessmen from the Qing Dynasty.

Walking on the flagstone lane lined by high walls and with gurgling streams underground, it seems you have entered a rural landscape picture. The village has been included into the UNESCO World Heritage List.

① A wood carving gate of the Wing Room in Chengzhi Hall

Dong Village in Zhaoxing, Liping (Ming and Qing: 1368-1911) – a Beautiful Mountain Village of Minority People in China

黎平肇兴侗寨(明清：1368—1911)——中国少数民族的美丽山寨

In southwest China, the Dong Village is 67 kilometers south of Liping County Seat in Guizhou Province. It is one of the famous villages of the Dong ethnic group in China and occupies an area of 180,000 square meters. It has a population of more than 4,000 living in more than 800 residential houses. The village has a beautiful surrounding with mountains around and a river passing through.

The Dong Village stands in a basin amid mountains. Rows upon rows of houses with high drum towers in the middle and fields and streams around constitute a beautiful traditional Chinese painting. All the houses in the village are pile dwellings built with fir logs and blue tiles. They look simple but neat. In the village there are theater halls, singing halls and grain houses, all in a good layout. The villagers belong to five families. So there are five drum towers, five flower bridges and five theater halls. The village is divided into five sections named Ren, Yi, Li, Zhi and Xing. The drum tower in the Zhi section is the most beautiful.

The drum towers are the most salient buildings of the village. Generally they are more than 10 meters tall with the tallest being some 20 meters. The tiled tower has double eaves and a top in a shape of a treasure bottle. It always has three or four stories and wooden stairs lead to the top of the tower. The drum tower is built with fir wood without any nails or rivets. It demonstrates a compact structure, a beautiful plastic art, excellent workmanship and elegant carvings and paintings. The drum tower is a place for villagers to meet and dis-

China's Rural Towns and Villages ■

cuss things, to have recreational activities and meet and send off their guests. The drum tower houses a drum which will be beaten by a senior to summon villagers when important events happen.

① Drum Tower of Dong Village
② A bird's-eys view of Dong Village in Zhaoxing
③ The Flower Bridge of Dong Village

* * * * * * * *

Danba Blockhouse Group (Ming and Qing: 1368-1911) – a Beautiful Mountainous Village of Minority People in China

丹巴碉楼群(明清：1368—1911)——中国少数民族的美丽山寨

The village with blockhouses is situated in Danba County, Sichuan Province in southwest China. These blockhouses were first built in 1700. According to their functions, they can be divided into three categories: military defensive blockhouses, government blockhouses and residential blockhouses built according to geomantic potency. Most blockhouses are quadrilateral, but some are pentagonal or hexagonal. Although they were built with slab-stones, their walls are solid and corners are straight. They are typical cultural architectures with features of river valleys in northwest Sichuan Province. The blockhouses in Suopo, Niexia, Badi, Jiaju and Geshizha townships are most distinguished.

First Group of Blockhouses 碉楼群 1 is seven kilometers north of Danba County Seat, mainly composed of the 13-Side Blockhouse.

Second Group of Blockhouses 碉楼群 2 is 10 kilometers north of Danba County Seat, mainly composed of Nuori Blockhouse, a 12-meter-high octagonal building with only half of it left.

Third Group of Blockhouses 碉楼

群 3 is 30 kilometers north of Danba County Seat, famous as the "valley of misses" for most Misses Kangba are from here.

① A group of blockhouses in Suopo Township
② A Tibet Mountainous village in Jiaju Township

Mushroom-Shaped Houses of Hani Ethnic Group and Yuanyang Terraced Fields (Ming and Qing: 1368-1911) – a Beautiful Mountainous Village of Minority People in China

哈尼族"蘑菇房"与元阳梯田(明清:1368—1911)——中国少数民族的美丽山寨

Such houses are found in the Honghe Hani-Yi Autonomous Prefecture in southwest China and other places. Hani is one of the 55 minority ethnic groups of China and has a population of 1.5 million. Hani ethnic group is famous for their mushroom-shaped houses and

terraced fields built in the several thousand years.

The Mushroom-shapde house 蘑菇房 Hani villages were always built on the half way up the mountains and the concentrated houses are laid out in a shape of mushroom. So these houses are called mushroom-shaped houses.

The Yuanyang terraced fields 元阳梯田 are the most typical and wonderful among those built on Ailao Mountain slopes. The terraced fields in the Tuguo Village and Qingkou Town lived by the Yi people at the spot of 5,000 meters from Yuanyang old county seat

to Luchun extend from the foot to the top of the mountain. In early spring, the fields are filled with water and, under the sunrise or sunset glow, the flying clouds above the fields change constantly and constitute various kinds of patterns. In summer and autumn, the mature and immature rice constitutes plots in natural colors, looking like a piece of nice oil painting.

The Hani villages and the terraced fields on the Ailao Mountain constitute a wonderful scene in rural areas.

The Earthen Houses in Fujian Province (Ming and Qing: 1368-1911) – Unmatched Residential Houses in the World

福建土楼(明清：1368-1911)——世界上独一无二的民居

Such earthen houses can be found in Yongding and Nanjing counties in Fujian Province in southeast China. During the Five Dynasties of more than 1,900 years ago, the central China suffered from frequent wars and the people moved to the south to avoid disasters brought by the wars. They moved several times and finally settled in the mountainous areas in southwest Fujian and became Hakkas. To avoid outside intrusion and bully, they had to live closely and built such a strong outer wall with local soil, sand, rocks and straw and constructed structure of houses and doors and windows with fir wood. They first built individual rooms and connected them into huge rooms and finally sealed their earthen houses.

Inside the roundhouse there are wells, grain warehouses. If a war or robbery occurred, they closed the gate and, if surrounded, maintained for several months with enough grains and water. Also such houses are warm in winter and cold in summer and can resist against earthquake and strong wind. The earthen houses became living places of Hakka people of one generation after another. Each earthen roundhouse is big enough for 70-80 families. They stand firmly for several hundred years and are a wonder of Chinese architecture of residential houses.

The earthen houses are of two big categories: round or square. The roundhouses are most unique. The earthen houses in Fujian Province are unique among Chinese residential houses and unmatched in the world history of architecture.

Chengqi House 乘启楼 in Gaotou Village, Yongding County, started to be built in the Chongzhen reign of the Ming Dynasty and was completed in 1709 or the 48th year of the Kangxi reign of the Qing Dynasty. This roundhouse is huge and has 400 rooms in four rings and is praised as the "king of the earthen roundhouses."

Zhencheng House 振成楼 in Hongkeng Village, Yongding County, was built in 1912.

It occupies an area of 5,000 square meters. This roundhouse was in an eight-diagram pattern. It has some 200 big or small rooms and is famous for elegant carvings. With a stage in its center the house can accommodate dozen thousand people to view the performance.

Kuiju House 奎聚楼 in Hongkeng Village, Yongding County, was built in 1834 and is a square earthen house of a palace-like structure, demonstrating the social position and power of the owner.

Tianluokeng Earthen House Group 田螺坑土楼群 is in Tianluokeng Village, Nanjing County, Fujian Province. The earthen houses in Tianluokeng Village were first built during the Ming Dynasty (1368-1644) and became popular during the Qing Dynasty (1644-1911). It was said some 600 years ago the Huangs moved here from Central Plains and lived on cultivation of ducks. The female ducks laid more quality eggs after eating snails (Tianluo in Chinese) in the fields. Since then the Huangs settled down. Since then the village got its name. In total there are five earthen houses in Tianluokeng, a square one in the middle and four roundhouses around. The 60-odd rooms in the square house are in two square rows with kitchens and dining halls on the first floor, warehouses on the second floor and bed rooms on the third floor. Ding Changsheng, a descendant of the Huang clan, built four roundhouses around the main square earthen house and named them "Hechang Buildings." Today, the Huang clan has more than 90 families with more than 500 members. A bird's-eye view shows that these earthen houses look like a plum blossom on a hilly terrace.

---

① Kuiju House
② Zhencheng House
③ Chengqi House
④ Tianluokeng Earthen House Group

✻   ✻   ✻   ✻   ✻   ✻   ✻   ✻

Zhujiajiao Town (Ming and Qing: 1368-1911) – a Small Town on the Outskirts of Shanghai

朱家角镇(明清：1368—1911)——大上海身边的小镇

This town is situated in southwestern part of Qingpu District, Shanghai. It has a population of 110,000 and is a famous historical and cultural town of Shanghai. Historical records show that it was the location of country fairs as early as in the Song Dynasty (960-1368) and became a village and got its name. The Zhujia Village developed into a town during the Wanli reign (1573-1620) of the Ming Dynasty and became a trade center in southern areas of the Yangtze River. It was famous for its production of Shanghai Rice Wine, quality rice and aquatic products. Three rivers run through the town. The houses and streets are concentrated by the Jingting Port. The streets and houses built during the Ming and Qing dynasties are intact today. Along the North Street, there were once thousand shops and the wooden buildings still reflect the flourishing of the town in the old days. The main scenic spots include botanic gardens, Wang Xu Ancestral Hall, Church, covered paths by the Jingting Port and Fangsheng Bridge. This bridge was first built during the Ming Dynasty (1368-1644) and was rebuilt in 1814 or the 19th year of the Jiaqing reign of the Qing Dynasty. It is the largest stone arch bridge in Shanghai areas.

In the past hundreds of years, Zhujiajiao was surrounded by water and the boats were the main transport means of the local residents. Such a unique natural condition turns the town a waterside village in the southern areas of the Yangtze River. Today the town has attracted flocks of Chinese and foreign tourists who think all things in the town are wonderful including the water, bridges, ancient streets, residential houses and even the food.

Marvels of China

Ancient Building Group in Wuyuan (Ming and Qing: 1368-1911) – China's Most Beautiful Village

婺源古建筑群(明清：1368－1911)——中国最美的乡村

This group of ancient buildings is located in Wuyuan County in northeastern part of Jiangxi Province in central China. The county covers an area of 2,947 square kilometers and has a population of 330,000. It has 18 townships or towns under its jurisdiction. Forests cover up to 82 percent of its total areas. The magnificent peaks, zigzagged rivers, fantastically-shaped rocks, ancient trees, flying waterfalls and plank paths constitute a painting of beautiful landscape. Ancient towns and villages of the Ming and Qing buildings can be seen everywhere in the county, composed of official mansions, former residences of celebrities, ancestral halls, local residential houses, and ancient streets and lanes paved with flagstones. In some villages or towns dozens of such buildings are linked together. In addition, there are stone arch bridges, covered bridges, roadside pavilions, gate towers, shop front and theaters. The residential houses with pink walls and blue tiles stand by the waters or at the foot of the green mountains. Such ancient buildings illustrate a combination of Chinese Confucian culture and the Anhui-style architectural art. The favorable ecological environment is the gift given to Wuyuan by nature while the good cultural background is the gift given to Wuyuan by the ancestors. When the rape comes into flower in March or April, it is the best season for touring Wuyuan.

Likeng Village 李坑村 is some 20 kilometers northeast of Wuyuan County Seat. The 260-odd-household village is a true portrayal of a waterside village with many bridges over the rivers.

Ancestral Hall of the Yu Clan in Wangkou Village 汪口村俞氏宗祠 is 30 kilometers northeast of Wuyuan County Seat. The Ancestral Hall of the Yu Clan was built during the Qing Dynasty. The flagstone-floored Ancestral Hall of the Yu Clan was built with 70 columns and occupies an area of more than 1,000 square meters. All the beams and brackets carry relief carvings on three sides. This ancestral hall is praised as an art treasure by experts.

Jingyi Hall of the Ancestral Temple of the Huang Clan in Huangcun Village 黄村黄氏宗祠经义堂 is 35 kilometers north of Wuyuan County and was built during the Kangxi reign of the Qing Dynasty. The hall was built with 100 fir columns, so it is also called "the 100-column ancestral hall." The roof beam bears delicate carvings and is decorated with traditional paintings of auspicious things in China. It was once exhibited in pho-

❷

tos in Paris in 1982 and shocked the viewers.

Maikeng Village 埋坑村 is 45 kilometers north of Wuyuan County Seat, in Tuochuan Township. It is one of the intact villages built during the Ming and Qing dynasties. The representative buildings in the village worth to visit are official residence of

3

Tiangong Shangqing, former residence of Sima, former government office and a building living by the people of nine generations. All these buildings have a stone gate, a terrazzo blue brick floor, and beams carved with flowers or figures from operas. The door and window carvings demonstrate unique and excellent workmanship. The village is one of historical and cultural ones in China.

① Maikeng Village
② The Ancestral Hall of the Yu Clan in Wangkou Village
③ Likeng Village

*   *   *   *   *   *   *   *

The Wang Family Compound (Qing: 1644-1911)
– China's First House

王家大院（清代：1644—1911）——被称为"中国第一宅"

This compound is located in Jingsheng Town, 12 kilometers east of Lingshi County Seat in central Shanxi Province, central China. Built by the Wang family during the Qing Dynasty, it occupies an area of 150,000 square meters. Of which 34,156 square meters are divided into three sections: Gaojiaya which houses the Museum of Chinese Dwellings and the Museum of the Wang Family, Hongmenpu and the Ancestral Hall of Filial Piety and Righteousness. In these three sections, there are 55 buildings with 1,083 rooms. Gaojiaya and Hongmenpu stand opposite to each other and are linked together through a bridge. All the castle-like buildings built on the loess

mounds according to the physical features stand in picturesque disorder, demonstrating a traditional style established during the Western Zhou (1046-771 B.C.) according to which the living area is located in front of sleeping area. But brick, wood and stone carvings as well as elegant decorations are rich in cultural contents. Also they are practical and beautiful, illustrating either south China or north China architectural styles. This family compound is praised as the gem of Chinese residential houses and China's first house.

Gaojiaya Building Group 高家崖建筑群 boasts 26 courtyards with 218 houses and covers an area of 11,728 square meters. The main courtyard boasts three small compounds with houses around. Each courtyard is composed of a tall ancestral hall flanked by two embroidery houses. Also each courtyard has an individual cooking yard and a clan school. But there are an academy of classical learning, gardening yard, hired laborers' yard and servants' yard. All buildings are walled in with doors opened in their suitable places. All the individual courtyards, the large or the small, are integrated into one. Of different sizes and with different functions, these courtyards like a mess, with one courtyard in another and one door stands behind another. All courtyards are decorated elegantly. All buildings are painted with auspicious things, illustrating a higher cultural quality.

Hongmenpu Building Group 红门堡建筑群 boasts 28 courtyards with 834 houses and covers an area of 19,800 square meters. All the buildings are arranged in a shape of a Chinese word " 王 ". Some courtyards are magnificent while others are small but quiet. Like Gaojiaya building group, all the houses and cave dwellings are well-proportioned. The carvings are delicate and dense, of the Qing style. The Museum of the Wang Family in this group has become a center for studying, displaying, collecting and developing the culture of the Wang clan at home and abroad.

*   *   *   *   *   *   *   *

The Qiao Family Compound (Qing: 1644-1911) – Imperial Palaces Among the People

乔家大院（清代：1644—1911）——被称为"中国民间皇宫"

It is in the Qiaojiapu Village, 10 kilometers northeast of Qixian County or 60 kilometers south of Taiyuan in Shanxi Province in central China. It is the former residence of Qiao Zhiyong from the third generation of the famous trade family of the Qiaos. It was first built in 1755 or the 20th year of the Qianlong reign of the Qing Dynasty and was expanded twice to become the largest residential compound in north China.

The Qiao Family Compound occupies an area of 8,724 square meters and has a floor space of 3,870 square meters. It is composed of six big courtyards and 19 small courtyards with a total of 313 houses, which fall into two groups in the south and north. The compound is like a castle circled by a 10-meter-high and one-meter-think wall. With a defensive function, it is like an imperial palace among ordinary people.

The six big courtyards are divided into two parts by a straight street. The main courtyards

are lived by the hosts and taller than the side courtyards which are for the guests or servants or are used as kitchens. The houses in the main courtyards have a tile roof and flying eaves while that in the side courtyards have a flat roof. On the flat roofs there are towers to tell hours or for looking far into the distance. The whole compound is well-proportioned. Even more than 140 chimneys are full of rhyming. The steps, doors, windows, eaves and rails in all courtyards are novel in their shapes. The stone, brick and wood carvings demonstrate a delicate workmanship. There is a saying, "Impe-

rial court owns the Museum of Palaces and the Qiao Family Compound is the representative of residential houses."

China's Rural Towns and Villages

Blockhouses in Kaiping (Qing-Republic of China: 1644-1949) – Residential Houses Represent a Combination of Chinese and Western Styles

开平碉楼（清代－民国：1644－1949）——中西结合的民居

❶

These blockhouses are located in Kaiping, south of Guangzhou in southeast China. They were first built in early years of the Qing Dynasty (1644-1911). The construction of such houses came to its climax in the 1920s and 1930s. Then many people from the southeast coastal areas left their hometown for other countries to make a living. They came back to their hometown and built such blockhouses in a unique Chinese-Western style with the money earned abroad. Such houses occupy a small area and can have many stories. They are solid to resist against flood and good to guard against theft. Such houses were fashionable then. Some overseas Chinese came back from Canada and built a village called the "Canadian Village." They are a typical example for making foreign things serve China.

These blockhouses fall into stone, hammed earthen or brick ones according to the building materials used. A few used reinforced concrete, the most advanced then. They were built in the classical Greek, Roman, Gothic and Islamic architectural styles. In Kaiping there are more than 1,833 intact blockhouses and are exotic flowers in the Chinese and Western architecture and become a wonder of the Chinese residential architecture.

Liyuan Garden 立园 is located in Genghua Village, 13 kilometers west of Kaiping City. It was a private garden-like villa

built in the 1920s by Xie Weili, a Chinese resided in the United States. It occupies 11,000 square meters and is composed of villa district, a large garden and a small garden.

Blockhouse Group in Zili Village 自力村碉楼群 is in Zili Village, 13 kilometers west of Kaiping City. In the village there are nine such blockhouses and six villas. The most famous ones are Longsheng Building, Mingshi Building, Maoshu Building and the Lantern Building of the Fang Family. Zili Village is a historical and cultural village famous in China.

Canadian Village 加拿大村 is on the outskirts of Chikan Town in Kaiping City.

Ruishi Building 瑞石楼 is located in Jinjiangli, Xiangang Town in Kaiping City. It was built in 1923 and is praised as the "first building in Kaiping."

Bianchou Building 边筹楼, or known as Xielou Building, is in Nanxing Village, Xiangang Town in Kaiping City. It was built in 1903 and is praised as the Leaning Tower of Pisa in Kaiping.

---

① Bianchou Building
② Ruishi Building
③ A group of blockhouses in Zili Village
④ Canadian Village
⑤ Liyuan Garden

Cave Dwellings in Yan'an (Republic of China: 1911-1949) – Dwellings of Red Power

Cave dwellings are in Yan'an area in northwest China. Such dwellings were built by the Chinese ancestors on the Loess Plateau and have a history of 4,000 or 5,000 years. Until today, there are 30-40 million Chinese people living in such cave dwellings. In general, cave dwellings were built on the sunny slope and are well-proportioned. Looked in distance,

they are magnificent. Each cave dwelling is six meters deep, four meters wide and falls into two categories: brick and earthen. They always have a semi-circular stone door and windows are decorated uniquely. Some cave dwellings are built in flat land with rocks and then covered with clay, a combination of stone and earthen cave dwelling styles. Cave dwell-

ings do not bring any damage to terrain and cultivated land and they are cheaper and cold in summer and warm in winter. The temperature inside is 13 degrees higher than outside in winter and 10 degrees lower in summer. But such cave dwellings have their shortcomings too. They do not have enough natural lighting inside and even wet in summer. Also they are bad ventilated.

Yan'an is one of the important centers for education in patriotism in China. From 1937 to 1947, the Chinese Communist Party Central Committee entered Yan'an and all leading members lived in such cave dwellings, slept on earthen beds and took millet as main staple food. Through arduous struggle and self-reliance, the Chinese Communist Party won victory in the revolution and established New China. Today Chinese and foreign people visit Yan'an and see the simple cave dwellings there and are impressed by the brilliant Yan'an spirit.

①The Former Residence of Mao Zedong at Zaoyuan in Yanan

Water Conservancy Projects in China

中国水利概述

China is rich in water resources and boasts many rivers. In total there are more than 1,500 rivers with a drainage area of 1,000 square kilometers or more each. In total China has 2,700 billion cubic meters of water, ranking the third in the world. Since ancient times, China has built many big or small dams across rivers in order to use the water to irrigate fields or generate power and created one wonder after another in the construction of water conservancy projects. In addition, China is one of the earliest countries to dig canals in the world. The south-north Grand Canal is a marvelous project in China and even in the world.

Dujiangyan (Warring States Period: 475-221 B.C.) – an Everlasting Water Conservancy Project

都江堰(战国:前 475- 前 221)——永远的水利工程

Dujiangyan is on the middle and upper reaches of the Minjiang River, 57 kilometers northwest of Chengdu in Sichuan Province in southwest China. This water project was built during the reign of King Qinzhao (306-251 B.C.) in the Warring States Period under the command of Li Bing, the governor of Shu Shrine. Today, it has a history of more than 2,200 years. The Minjiang River originates from the southern foot of Minshan Mountain in Songpan County, Sichuan Province. It joins other rivers and runs down with great amounts of sands to the plains. So it is always blocked by sands and brings a lot of disasters to the people on both banks. The governor of Shu Shrine Li Bing led his people to cut the Yulei

1

Water Conservancy Projects in China

Pavilion, tourists can have a bird's-eye view of the Anlan Cable Bridge, Fish's Mouth and Xiling Snow-Clad Peak.

Two Kings Temple 二王庙 is at the foot of the Yulei Mountain on the east bank of the Minjiang River. It was built during the Southern and Northern Dynasties(420-589) in the memory of Li Bing and his son, the builders of Dujiangyan Irrigation System. The present-day temple was rebuilt during the Qing Dynasty and houses the statues of Li Bing and his son. The temple was built according to the terrain of the mountain and the red halls and pavilions in it have upturned eaves. Standing on the bank of the river, it is magnificent.

Stone Statue of Li Bing 李冰石像 is housed in the Great Hall of the Fulong Taoist Temple and was built in 168 or the first year of the Jianning reign of the Eastern Han Dynasty. The statue is 2.9 meters high and weighs 4.5 tons. In the breast there is an inscription and the date of its building. The statue was discovered in the center of the river in 1974 and is one of the rare historical relics of Dujiangyan.

Mountain in order to lead the river down through two courses according to the geographic conditions of being higher in northwest of west Sichuan than in southeast. The 700-kilometer-long outer river is the main course and the river empties into the Yangtze River while the inner river is actually a man-made tunnel and runs to the Chengdu Plain, thus either avoiding the disasters or irrigating the fields around. This project has brought benefits to the people of one generation after another and until today it is still in function. It has been the permanent and the oldest irrigation project in the world and has been included into the World Heritage List by the UNESCO.

Fulong Taoist Temple 伏龙观 is located in Lidui Park, by the Baoping Sluiceway and at the foot of the Lidui Hill and is a memorial building. It was first built during the Jin Dynasty (256-420). A legend says Li Bing and his son controlled evil dragon of the Minjiang River and locked it at the bottom of the Fulong Lake while bringing the river under the control. In the Scene-Viewing

---

① Dujiangyan Water Conservancy Project
② A stone statue of Li Bing
③ Two Kings Temple
④ Fish's Mouth
⑤ Fulong Taoist Temple

Karez Irrigation System (Western Han-Present: 206 B.C.-Present) – the Longest Subterranean Canal in the World

坎儿井（西汉至今：前206至今）——世界上最长的地下运河

This irrigation system is distributed in Turpan and Hami areas in Xinjiang, northwest China. It was built by the people according to the local climate and hydrological conditions in basin areas. This irrigation system has a history of more than 2,000 years.

The Turpan area has a rainfall of only 16 mm a year but its evaporation is 3,000 mm. It is impossible to use the water in the surface to irrigate farmland. Fortunately, Turpan is located in a basin and the mountains around are covered by snow year round so the area is rich in water resources underground. Therefore the local people brought into full play the tilted terrain of the basin and dug many karez and connected them together into a subterranean irrigation system.

Such irrigation system has a simple structure but the whole project is hard to build. First many vertical wells were dug at an interval of 10 meters or several dozen meters. These wells were connected through a canal underground. The sands and stones from the shafts or canal were piled around the mouth of the well, like a small crate in distance. The vertical wells have different depths according to the slope of the canal. The water will automatically flow to the outlets on the faraway oases. Then the water is led to the ditches on the ground and finally to the farmland. In general the karez is three kilometers long and

the longest 10 kilometers. In Turpan, you can see horses are drinking the water from such karez on the Gobi deserts. Historical records show this longest irrigation system once totaled more than 5,000 kilometers.

Such irrigation system is a symbol of oasis civilization of Xinjiang. Its ecological and cultural values are irreplaceable. Karez irrigation system is praised as the longest subterranean canal in the world.

✳   ✳   ✳   ✳   ✳   ✳   ✳   ✳

The Grand Canal (Sui-Yuan: 518-1368) – a Great Project Next to the Great Wall

大运河(隋代－元代：518－1368)——仅次于长城的伟大工程

The Grand Canal is in the north-south area of east China. China is the earliest country for constructing the canal in the world. As early as in the late years of the Spring and Autumn Period (around 485 B.C.), the Fangou Canal, a man-made river, was dug in the present-day Yangzhou by the State of Wu to connect the Yangtze River and Huaihe River. It was 150 kilometers long and was the first canal in the world. From the first to the sixth year (605-610) of the Daye reign of the Sui Dynasty, a south-north grand canal was built through hard work with Luoyang, then the capital city, as the center. It was 2,700 kilometers long and was famous as the south-north canal built by Emperor Tangdi of the Sui

Dynasty. During the Yuan Dynasty (1271-1368), the Beijing-Hangzhou Grand Canal was built based on this south-north canal with Beijing as the center. This Grand Canal passed through Tianjin, Hebei, Shandong, Jiangsu, and Zhejiang and is 1,794 kilometers long and is 30-70 meters wide. It is 16 times the length of the Suez Canal, or 33 times that of the Panama Canal. It connects the Haihe, Yellow, Huaihe, Yangtze and Qiantang rivers together. At present, the Beijing-Hangzhou Grand Canal is opened to traffic for 1,442 kilometers including 877 kilometers opened year round. The main sections opened to traffic are concentrated in Shandong, Jiangsu and Zhejiang provinces, in the southern areas of the Yellow

River.

The construction of the Grand Canal has benefited the exchange of goods between the northern and southern areas and helped the political, economic and cultural development of China. After the founding of New China in 1949, Chinese government has carried large-scale repairs of the Grand Canal on several occasions. Along the Grand Canal great amounts of cultural and historical sites have been found

and the canal itself is praised as a long corridor of ancient water culture of China. Recently several museums on the Grand Canal have been established along the canal. Not as eye-catching as the Great Wall and Terra-Cotta Warriors, this Grand Canal is still in use. Some itineraries have been developed in the sections of Hangzhou, Suzhou and Wuxi and are welcomed by Chinese and foreign tourists. The Grand Canal is as wonderful as the Great Wall and is a marvelous event in Chinese water conservancy construction and a wonder in the world.

Marvels of China

Red Flag Irrigation Ditch (New China: 1949-Present) – the Man-Made River in China

红旗渠（新中国：1949 至今）——中国的"人工天河"

meters long main ditches and 4,013.6 kilometers long tributary ditches for leading water to the fields. Also they constructed 396 small and medium-sized reservoirs and ponds. They brought into full play the natural drop and built 45 small hydropower stations. Also they constructed a large-scale water system with an aim to lead, store and raise water for irrigation, drainage,

This ditch is in Linzhou City, Henan Province in central China. Its construction lasted for more than nine years, from February 1960 to July 1969. The water originates from the Zhuozhang River and is blocked by a dam in Pingshun County in Shanxi Province. Then the water from the river is led to Linzhou in Henan Province. Almost for 10 years, 100,000 laborers relied on their own efforts, dug tunnels on mountains and built bridges over the mountain valleys. In total, they leveled 1,250 mountain tops, built 152 aqueducts, dug 211 tunnels and finally built 70.6 kilo-power generation and tourism. The local laborers built 12,408 buildings of various kinds, dug 22.25 million cubic meters of earth and stone. If a two-meter-high and three-meter-wide wall built with these earth and stone, the wall can run from Harbin in northeast China to Guangzhou in south China. The project has put an end to the history in which Linzhou was hit by drought nine of 10 years and has fundamentally changed the production and living conditions of local people. This ditch is praised as a ditch of life, happy ditch or man-made river by the local people.

Three Gorges Project (New China: 1949-Present) – the World's Largest Hydropower Station

三峡工程(新中国:1949 至今)──世界最大的水电站

This hydropower project is on the Yangtze River, 38 kilometers west of Yichang City, Hubei Province in central China. The construction started in 1992 and its main part was completed on May 20, 2006. The whole project is planned to complete in three phases or 18 years. The first-phase project lasted for five years from 1992 to 1997, the second-phase project lasted for six years from 1998 to 2003 and the third-phase project is planned

1

to complete in 2009, lasting for six years. After the dam was completed the water level can be raised to 100 meters and the reservoir will be 600 kilometers long and 2,000 meters wide at maximum, covering an area of 10,000 square kilometers.

The Three Gorges Project is composed of the dam, hydropower station and navigation buildings. The axis of the dam is 2,309.47 meters long (the top of the dam is 3,035 meters long) and 185 meters high. The hydropower station is equipped with 26 700,000-kw generators, with an installed generating capacity of 18.2 million kwh. The annual generating capacity totals 84.68 billion kwh. The sluice gate has its maximum capacity of 102,500 cubic meters per second. The navigation facilities are composed of a permanent ship lock and a ship-raising machine.

The construction of the Three Gorges

Project has made the dream of the Chinese people into true. The project has played a strong beneficial role in flood prevention, power generation and navigation. As a result, its construction has freed 15 million local people and 1.5 million hectares of farmland from floods. The hydropower station has produced half of electricity China needs. The navigation condition of the river has improved greatly so that the 10,000-ton-class ships can run from Shanghai directly to Chongqing. The Three Gorges Project is a new Great Wall Project built by the Chinese people and is one of the wonders in the construction of water conservancy projects in the world.

Appendix: The Three Gorges Project leads in the following 10 fields:

附：三峡工程创造的10个世界之最

The largest construction scale 建筑规模最大：The axis of the dam is 2,309.47 meters long and the waterway dam is 483 meters long. It is equipped with 26 generators with 700,000-kw each, double-way five-step ship lock and ship-raising machine. All these show that the project is of the largest scale of its kind in the world in individual project or the Three Gorges Project as a whole.

The largest engineering amount 工程量最大：For the main project 134 million cubic meters of earth and stone were dug and 27.94 million cubic meters of concrete and 463,000 tons of reinforced bars were used.

The most difficult project 施工难度最大：The year of 2000 registered a world record of using a total of 5.4817 million cubic meters of concrete, averaging 550,000 cubic meters a month.

The largest hydropower station 最大的电站：The total installed generating capacity totals 18.2 million kwh with an annual generating capacity being 84.68 billion kwh.

The largest rate of flow during the

construction period 施工期流量最大： The rate of flow after the river was blocked reached 9,010 cubic meters per second. The rate of flow when the river water was led during the construction topped 79,000 cubic meters per second.

The sluice gate with the largest flood discharge 泄洪能力最大的泄洪闸： Its sluice gate has a discharge capacity of 102,500 cubic meters of water per second.

The inland river ship lock with the most steps and highest top step 级数最多、总水头最高的内河船闸: The project has five-step double-way ship lock and the highest water level at the top step.

The largest and most difficult ship-raising machine 规模最大、难度最高的升船机: The effective size of the ship-raising machine is 120 x 18 x 3.5 meters. The highest level it can lift the ship to is 113 meters. The lock together with water weighs 11,800 tons and the ships to be lifted are of the class of 3,000 tons.

The obvious flood-prevention efficiency 防洪效益最显著： The Three Gorges Reservoir has a storage capacity of 39.3 billion cubic meters and that for preventing flood is 22.15 billion cubic meters. The flow for regulating the flood peak is 27,000-33,000 cubic meters per second, big enough to effectively control the flood water on the upper reaches of the Yangtze River and improve the ability to prevent the flood on the middle and lower reaches of the river.

The most migrates moving away from the reservoir area 水库移民最多: Finally, a total of 1.13 million people have to move off the reservoir area, making the project one with the most arduous migration task.

---

① The Three Gorges Project
② The locals moving away from the Three Gorges Area
③ The magnificent scene of the flood discharge of the Three Gorges Dam

Chinese Bridges

中国桥梁概述

China is a country with more rivers, mountains and canyons. Bridges in various parts are of great numbers and great varieties. For the materials used, the bridges can be divided into wood, bamboo, stone or brick, glazed, iron and steel, glass and reinforced concrete. For shapes, they can be divided into pontoon, cable, boat, arch, pavilion, roofed, veranda-like, multi-span, and overpass bridges. Many bridges become wonders in Chinese history of bridge construction for their long history, unique shape, novel structure or huge scale.

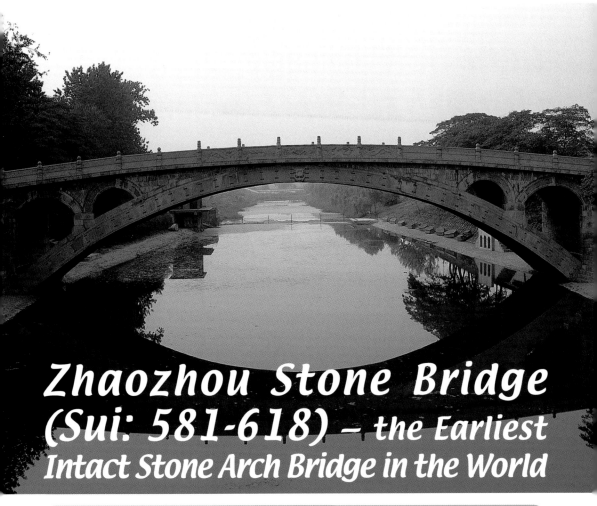

Zhaozhou Stone Bridge (Sui: 581-618) – the Earliest Intact Stone Arch Bridge in the World

赵州大石桥(隋代：581-618)——世界现存最早的石拱桥

Over the Jiaohe River 45 kilometers southeast of Shijiazhuang in Hebei Province, north China, the Zhaozhou Bridge was built during 605-615 or the first year to 11th year of the Daye reign of the Sui Dynasty. Designed by Li Chun, this arch bridge has one span. It is 50.82 meters long and 9.6 meters wide and was built with 28 pieces of arch rocks. The net span is 37.02 meters. On each of the two shoulders of the main arch there are two spandrel arches. Its delicate design lessons the obstruction from the water and also reduces the pressure from the bridge itself. The design of its open shoulders wrote a new chapter in history of world bridge architecture and is an important contribution the Chinese working people have made to the world science and technology. In October 1991, the US Civil Engineers Society selected the Zhaozhou Bridge the 12th milestone of international civil engineering history. The sign erected by the bridge has added luster to Chinese architecture of bridges.

Gem Belt Bridge in Suzhou (Tang: 618-907) – a Towing Path

苏州宝带桥(唐代：618—907)——中国背纤人走的桥

On the bank of the Grand Canal some seven kilometers southeast of Suzhou in Jiangsu Province, in east China, the Gem Belt Bridge was first built during 816-819 or from the 11th year to the 14th year of the Yuanhe reign of the Tang Dynasty. It was said the bridge was built with the money from the gem belt donated by Wang Zhongshu, a regional chief from the Tang Dynasty. So it has the name. Today, the major buildings were built in 1872 or the 11th year of the Tongzhi reign of the Qing Dynasty. This stone bridge has 53 spans and is 317 meters long and 4.1 meters wide. This bridge was built for the people who towed boats and is not as steep and tall as common arch stone bridges in southern areas of the Yangtze River. This bridge is multi-span, narrow and smooth and a wonder in history of bridge architecture in China and even in the world.

Lugou Bridge in Beijing (Jin: 1115-1234) – Known as Marco Polo Bridge Among Westerners

北京卢沟桥（金代：1115–1234）──西方人称其为"马可·波罗桥"

It is over the Yongding River 18 kilometers southwest of Beijing proper. Because the Yongding River was called Lugou River in the old days, so the bridge got its name. The bridge was first built in 1189 or the 29th year of the Dading reign of the Jin Dynasty. It was destroyed during a flood and was rebuilt in 1698 or the 37th year of the Kangxi reign of the Qing Dynasty. It is 267 meters long and nine meters wide and has 11 arches, the longest stone bridge built in ancient times in north China. The Lugou Bridge enjoys a great reputation at home and abroad for following reasons:

"As uncountable as the lions of Lugou Bridge" is a common expression around Beijing. Its stone balustrades have 140 sculptured balusters on either side with a lion carved on the top of each, each lion being different in posture from the others. According to a survey the cultural relic workers made in the 1960s shows that there are 485 lions. An-

other survey made in the 1980s shows the figure is 498. Today the people say there are 501 lions including three ones found in the river later.

It is known as the Marco Polo Bridge among European and American tourists. Italian traveler Marco Polo (1254-1324) praised the bridge in his travel notes as "the most wonderful and unique bridge in the world". So this bridge has been known in the world as early as several hundreds of years ago.

It was here that the curtain rose on the Chinese people's great war of resistance to Japanese aggression in 1937 with what is known as the Lugou Bridge Incident of July 7.

✳   ✳   ✳   ✳   ✳   ✳   ✳   ✳

Anping Bridge in Quanzhou (Southern Song: 1127-1279) – the Longest Stone Beam Bridge in Ancient China

泉州安平桥(南宋：1127－1279)──中国古代最长的石梁桥

This bridge connects Anhai Town in Jinjiang City and Shuitou Town in Nan'an City in Fujian Province in southeast China. It was first built in 1138 or the eighth year of the Chaoxing reign of the Southern Song Dynasty and was completed 13 years later. The bridge is 3,070 meters long and is the longest stone beam bridge in ancient China. It was built with slab stones which are 8-11 meters long, 0.5-1 meter thick and five tons in weight each. On the bridge, there are Shuixin Pavilion, Central Pavilion, Palace Pavilion, Rain Pavilion and Building-like Pavilion for the people to take a rest. Also the bridge has stone balustrades and sculptured balusters on either side with generals, lions or toads on each. In water on either side of the bridge there are four square stone towers and one round tower, symmetrically. The white tower by the entrance to the bridge is

22 meters tall. This five-story hexagon hollow tower demonstrates a simple and ancient architectural style. This rainbow-like bridge is magnificent. During the Song and Yuan dynasties here was bustling and an important seaport of ancient Quanzhou.

The Anping Bridge is famous at home and abroad as "the longest one of its kind in the world" and is a wonder in the Chinese architecture of ancient bridges.

✻ ✻ ✻ ✻ ✻ ✻ ✻ ✻

An Acute-Angle-Shaped Bridge in Shaoxing (Southern Song: 1127-1279) – the Earliest Overpass in China

绍兴八字桥(南宋：1127−1279)——中国最早的立交桥

In Shaoxing, Zhejiang Province, east China, this overpass is an ancient beam-shaped stone bridge. It was first built in 1256 or the fourth year of the Baoyou reign of the Southern Song Dynasty. Actually it is composed of two bridges which join at one end to make an acute angle, so the name of the bridge. The bridge crosses the south-north main river and the two small ones on its both sides and links four roads together. The originator of the Chinese overpasses, it was built with blue stones. The curved slab stones for the main section of the bridge are 4.85 meters long each. Also it has stone balustrades and balusters. One of a few intact bridges from the Song Dynasty, this ancient arch bridge which has solved such a complicated traffic problem is really a wonder in the Chinese architecture of bridges.

* * * * * * * *

Covered Bridge in Taishun (Ming:1368-1644) – a Multi-Function Bridge from Ancient China

泰顺廊桥（明代：1368-1644）——中国古代的多功能桥

This bridge is in Taishun County in Zhejiang Province in southeast China. Taishun County is imbued with mountains and deep valleys. Local people had to build roads across mountains and bridges over rivers. Originally there were some 1,000 covered bridges but only more than 470 of them are intact today. The county is famous as a museum of ancient bridges of China. Most bridges in the county are wooden and each has wooden houses on. On either side of the bridge, there are fixed wooden chairs. Some even have a sacrificial table, a tea pavilion or a guest room. Such bridge is seldom in China and attracts flocks of tourists or inspectors in recent years.

Liu Family Bridge 刘宅桥 is in Sangui Town in Taishun County. It was built in 1405 or the third year of the Yongle reign of the Ming Dynasty. The house on the bridge has six bays supported by 45 pillars. The wooden house can keep off the sunlight and rain and resist rust. Also it can provide a place for the people to take a rest.

Dongxi Bridge or Upper Bridge 东溪桥（又称上桥） is in Sixi Town in Taishun County. It was first built in 1570 or the fourth year of the Longqing reign of the Ming Dynasty. It is 41.7 meters long, 4.86 meters wide and 10.35 meters tall. Its span is 25.7 meters long. This arch bridge has a palace-like house with upturned corners and double eaves. The house is magnificent and elegant.

Beixi Bridge or Lower Bridge 北溪桥（又称下桥）is in Sixi Town in Taishun County. The Lower Bridge is wider and taller than the Upper Bridge and

its span is longer too. Looked in distance, the Beixi Bridge is like a beautiful curve over the blue water. In the eyes of cultural relic experts, it is "the first of its kind in the southern area of the Yangtze River" and "a unique national treasure".

✻   ✻   ✻   ✻   ✻   ✻   ✻   ✻

Luding Bridge in Sichuan (Qing: 1644-1911) – the Life and Death Bridge on the Long March of the Red Army

四川泸定桥（清代：1644–1911）——红军长征路上的生死桥

It is over the Dadu River to the west of Luding County in Sichuan Province in southwest China. The construction of this suspended cable bridge started in 1705 or the 44th year of the Kangxi reign of the Qing Dynasty and was completed five years later. The bridge is 101 meters long and three meters wide. The bridge floor is 14.5 meters above the lower water level. It is supported by 13 iron chains – nine horizontal ones connected with the two

has been an important passage linking Sichuan with the Sichuan-Tibet Plateau.

On May 29, 1935, the Chinese Workers and Peasants Red Army arrived here during its Long March. Its 22-member advance team climbed forward along this chain bridge under the gun fire and eliminated the defensive enemy. After the team controlled the bridge the Red Army forces crossed the Dadu River and threw off the chasing KMT troops. The Red Army forces created miracles in Chinese military history. Since then the Luding Bridge has become known in the world. Today it is one of the famous tourist destinations of China.

banks and floored with wooden planks and two ones on either side of the bridge as balustrades. Each chain is 2.5 tons in weight. In more than 300 years in the past, this bridge

*   *   *   *   *   *   *   *

Five-Pavilion Bridge in Yangzhou (Qing: 1644-1911) – a Combination of Power and Beauty

扬州五亭桥(清代:1644—1911)——被誉为力与美的结合

Across the Lesser West Lake in Yangzhou, Jiangsu Province in east China, this bridge was built in 1757 or the 22nd year of the Qianlong reign of the Qing Dynasty by the salt businessmen for welcoming Emperor Qianlong. For five pavilions on it, the bridge has its name. A bird's-eye view shows the five pavilions on the bridge look like a lotus. So the bridge is called the Lotus Bridge too. Today it is a new symbol of Yangzhou.

The Five-Pavilion Bridge is 55.3 meters long. Having stone steps on both ends, the bridge has 12 stone piers and 15 arches of three kinds. The longest span is 7.13 meters long. The five pavilions on the bridge are linked together by roofed short passages. The square central pavilion has double eaves, a tile pavilion roof and four upturned corners. The square lower part of these beautiful pavilions represents the square earth and the round top symbolizes the round sky. These five pavilions have yellow tiles, red pillars and white balustrades. The colorful caisson ceiling of the pavilions is elegant. In the night, the reflections of the bridge and the moon in the water constitute a wonderful scene. Some people call the piers as brave soldiers and pavilions as beautiful girls. So the bridge represents a harmonious combination of power and beauty and magnificence and delicacy. It is a miracle in the Chinese architecture of bridges.

*   *   *   *   *   *   *   *

Yongji Bridge in Chengyang (Republic of China: 1911-1949)
– a Symbol of Dong Architecture

程阳永济桥(民国：1911–1949)——侗族建筑的象征

Also known as the Wind and Rain Bridge, the Yongji Bridge is in Chengyang Village, 20 kilometers north of Sanjiang Dong Autonomous County in Guangxi Zhuang Autonomous Region in south China. It was built in 1916 and was rebuilt twice after being destroyed by floods. The current bridge was rebuilt two years after it was destroyed by flood in June 1983.

It is a wooden covered bridge and is 76 meters long, 3.4 meters wide and 10.6 meters tall. It has five stone piers on which are two

rows of log beams and two rows of wood suspension beams. On the bridge floor there are five tower-like kiosks with many horns. The kiosks on both ends have a gable roof with upturned corners, like golden phoenix with spread wings. The kiosk in the middle has a pavilion-like roof and six upturned corners, like a solemn but elegant pagoda. The rest two kiosks have a pavilion-like roof with four upturned corners, like a magnificent palace each. On both sides of the bridge long stools were set up for people to rest or keep off the rain. The whole bridge is grand, like a brilliant rainbow, The most amazing thing is that no nails were used in its construction. In addition, the kiosks and roofed corridors are painted with colorful patterns of local style. The Yongji Bridge in Chengyang symbolizes the superb architectural art of the Dong minority people and is a miracle created by the local people.

* * * * * * * *

Bamboo Bridge of Va Ethnic Group – Primitive Bridge Rarely Seen in China

佤族竹桥——中国罕见的原始桥

This bamboo bridge is in Ximeng County   in west Yunnan Province in southwest China.

arrows, fish with bamboo baskets, carry cereals with bamboo baskets and keep counts with bamboo strips. Especially they built bamboo bridges. They tie two iron chains to the big trees on two banks of the river and bamboo sticks are hung from iron chains and every two bamboo sticks are tied together at their other end, making a Y-shape bridge. Then several wooden logs were put on as the bridge floor in the convenience of people to walk on it. The bamboo bridge is so simple and is a miracle. As local economy has developed such bamboo bridges are seldom to see.

Va ethnic group is one of the 55 minority groups in China and has a population of 370,000. The Va people are mainly living in Ximeng, Cangyjan, Menglian, Gengma and Lancang counties in Yunnan Province. These places are imbued with bamboo and the bamboo culture has become a traditional cultural feature of the Va people. The Va people live in bamboo buildings, plant seeds with bamboo sticks, hunt with bamboo bows and

Bamboo Bridge over Nankang River 南亢河佤族竹桥 is in Lisuo Township in Ximeng County. It is also known as the Zuokuo Bridge among local people.

Nanjing Bridge over the Yangtze River – a Pride of the Chinese People

南京长江大桥——值得中国人骄傲的现代化大桥

This bridge is in Nanjing, Jiangsu Province in east China. The construction started in 1960

and completed and put into traffic by the end of 1968. It is a modern bridge over the Yangtze River designed and built by the Chinese people.

Before the 1990s, this was the longest double-deck rail and road bridge. The main section is 1,577 meters long. If the approaches to the rail section are included the rail bridge is 6,772 meters long. The rail bridge has double tracks for two-way trains. The road bridge is 4,589 meters long including the approaches and is 19.5 meters wide, enough for four trucks abreast. The main part over the river has nine piers and 10 spans. Each pier is 80 meters high and the bottom of the pier covers an area of more than 400 square meters. The first span from left is 128 meters long

and the rest nine spans are 160 meters long each. The four bridge towers on two ends are more than 70 meters tall and by the bridge towers there are four groups of sculptures being more than 10 meters tall. The approaches to the road bridge have 34 spans in total – 30 spans on the southern bank and four spans on northern bank. This bridge symbolizes a national feature.

Before its completion, it took two hours for the train to be shipped across the river. The construction of the bridge has played an important role in link of north and south China and the construction of the country. It is a miracle in construction history of Chinese bridges.

Chinese Museums

中国博物馆概述

China has more than 2,000 museums at the national, provincial and city levels. In the past few years many private museums have opened in various parts of the country. The museums are of great varieties and their sponsors are from different social strata. Even the 12 provinces and autonomous regions in comparatively poor west China boast more than 400 museums of various kinds, ending the situation in which the museums were concentrated in medium-sized and large cities in central and east China.

According to their nature, these museums fall into two categories: comprehensive and thematic. The comprehensive ones are museums of local history. The thematic ones are museums of natural sciences, art, geology, science and technology, agriculture, military, architecture, textile, silk, tea, literature, sports, folk customs, and ancient tombs. In the past few years a group of private museums have been emerged such as those of traditional Chinese medicines, furniture, abacus, clocks and watches, postal stamps, currencies, chopsticks, clothing and kites. In addition, there are former residences of celebrities from various historical stages. Here we list some distinguished ones.

Palace Museum in Beijing with the Richest Cultural Relics

北京故宫博物院——收藏文物最丰富的博物馆

The Palace Museum in the center of Beijing is a comprehensive museum expanded from the imperial palaces of and the collections from the Ming and Qing dynasties. For its architecture please see the chapter on Chinese palaces. Here we introduce you the collections of cultural relics the museum houses.

The Palace Museum collects more than one million pieces of ancient literary and art materials, one sixth of China's total cultural relics. In addition to the living articles used by Ming and Qing emperors and their wives, papers and documents from the two dynasties,

there are bronzes, jades, paintings and calligraphic works, ceramics, enamels, lacquer ware, golden and silver articles, Chinese and foreign clocks and watches. These cultural relics have great value for the study of Chinese history, culture and art. After the founding of New China, state allocation, collection from society and individuals' donations have increased the collection of the cultural relics by some 220,000 pieces, filling many blanks in the collections. Especially the collections of ancient paintings and calligraphic works include calligraphic works by Lu Ji and Wang

Xun from the Jin Dynasty, *On the Goddess of the Luo River* by Gu Kaizhi from the Jin Dynasty, *On Tours in Spring* by Zhan Ziqian from the Sui Dynasty, *Five Oxen* 《五牛图》 by Han Huang and *Poems by Zhang Haohao* by Du Mu from the Tang Dynasty, *Han Xizai at a Night Feast* 《韩熙载夜宴图》 by Gu Hongzhong and *The Festival of Pure Brightness on the River* 《清明上河图》 by Zhang Zeduan from the Five Dynasties. All these calligraphic works and paintings are gem of China.

Exhibitions in the Palace Museum fall into two categories: exhibitions of imperial courts in their original forms and various kinds of art treasures related and thematic exhibitions.

The first category includes ceremonies to show how the emperor holds court, the emperor reads and comments on a document, and the life of the emperor and his wife. The thematic exhibitions include those to display the arts from various historical periods, bronzes, ceramics, paintings, gems, clocks and watches, documents and cultural relics from Qing Dynasty, and opera-related cultural relics from Qing Dynasty. The Palace Museum houses the largest collection of cultural relics in China and is famous for its collection of ancient culture and art in the world. Many of them are invaluable cultural relics and the only ones in the world.

① *Han Xizai at a Night Feast*
② *Five Oxen*

Shanghai Museum – a Museum of Ancient Chinese Art

At 201 People's Road and at the southern end of the People's Square, Shanghai Museum is a large museum of ancient Chinese art. It was opened in 1952 and moved here in 1994. The new museum has a floor space of 38,000 square meters and has five stories above the ground and two stories under the ground. It has a square base and a round top, symbolizing the ancient Chinese philosophy that the square earth is under the round sky. Shanghai Museum houses a collection of one million cultural relics, especially the bronzes, ceramics, and calligraphic works and paintings. It embraces 11 thematic exhibition rooms, one hall for displaying donated cultural relics and three exhibition halls. It has an actual exhibition area of 12,000 square meters. On the first floor are Exhibition Room of Ancient Chinese Bronzes, Exhibition Room of Ancient Chinese Sculptures and an exhibition hall. On the second floor are the Exhibition Room of Ancient Chinese Ceramics, the Exhibition Room of Modern Chinese Ceramics and an exhibition hall. On the third floor are the Exhibition Room of Chinese Calligraphic Works from Various Historical Periods, the Exhibition Room of Chinese Paintings from Various Historical Periods and

the Exhibition Room of Chinese Seals from Various Historical Periods. On the fourth floor are the Exhibition Room of Ancient Chinese Jade, the Exhibition Room of Ancient Chinese Currencies and Coins, the Exhibition Room of Chinese Furniture from the Ming and Qing Dynasties, the Exhibition Room of Handicrafts of Various Ethnic Groups in China and an exhibition hall. In addition there are two temporary halls. The museum is famous for its rich and complete collections of cultural relics of high grades at home and abroad. Such as the great three- or four-legged cauldrons from the Western Zhou Dynasty, the crabapple-shaped bowl of the Yue kiln from the Tang Dynasty, *Ya Tou Wan Calligraphic Works on Silk* 《鸭头丸帖》by Wang Xianzhi from the Eastern Jin Dynasty, Painting *Recluse* by Sun Wei from the Tang Dynasty are all rare cultural relics.

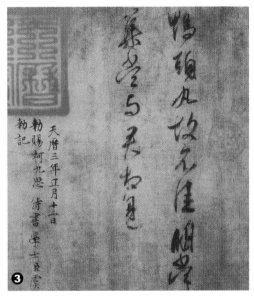

① The Greater Bronze Vessel
② Gong Fu Yi *gong* (ancient bronze wine vessel) of the late Shang Dynasty
③ *Ya Tou Wan Calligraphic Works on Silk*

Shanghai Museum has organized exhibitions of its collections of cultural relics in foreign countries and sponsored international academic research forums. Also it has published books and periodicals on archaeological findings and cultural relics. In addition, the museum has established offices in charge of cultural exchanges, archaeology and repairing of cultural relics.

Hunan Provincial Museum
– Famous for the Display of
Mawangdui Han Tomb

湖南省博物馆——因马王堆汉墓而闻名于世

The Hunan Provincial Museum is situated in Changsha City, Hunan Province in central China and is one of the historical and artistic one at the provincial level. It covers an area of 50,000 square meters with a floor space of 20,000 square meters. Its construction started in March 1951 and completed and opened to the public in February 1956. Today the museum contains a collection of more than 110,000 objects, mainly of which are bronzes from the Shang and Zhou dynasties and lacquer ware from the State of Chu.

After the Mawangdui Han Tomb was found in 1972, the museum built a 10,000-square-meter theme exhibition hall for displaying more than 3,000 rare relics and corpse exca-vated from the three Han tombs in Mawangdui. The T-shaped silk picture found in the Mawangdui No. 1 Han Tomb is 2.05 meters long, supposedly a banner for the soul. It describes the voyage from the dead to the next world. Twenty-eight long-lost ancient silk books were unearthed in the Mawangdui No. 3 Han Tomb, most of which are of great medicinal, astronomical, philosophical and historical values, including *Laozi, The Book of Changes, Political Strategists of the Warring States Period, Prognostications Related to the Five Planets, Prognostications Related to the Astronomy and Meteorology,* and *Prescriptions for Fifty-Two Kinds of Diseases.* The cultural relics unearthed in the

Mawangdui Han Tombs in Changsha and other rare relics have been exhibited in Hong Kong and other parts of the country and even in Japan, the United States and other countries and regions and received high appreciation from Chinese and foreign viewers.

✳ ✳ ✳ ✳ ✳ ✳ ✳ ✳

Forest of Steles in Xi'an – the Most Ancient Treasure House of Stone Carved Calligraphic Works in the World

西安碑林——被誉为世界最古的石刻书库

1

On Sanxue Street in Xi'an City, northwest China, the Forest of Steles was the location of Confucian Temple. It was built in 1087 or the second year of the Yuanyou reign of the Northern Song Dynasty to keep *Thirteen Classics* carved in the Kaicheng reign of the Tang Dynasty. It has been expanded step by step and developed into a forest of steles in early

Qing Dynasty (1644-1911). Today it has seven exhibition halls, six galleries and one stele pavilion. On display are more than 1,000 carved steles from different historical periods from the Han Dynasty (206-220 B.C.) to the Qing Dynasty (1644-1911). They are excellent works by famous calligraphers from various historical periods and are one of China's treasure houses of calligraphic art. The most valuable ones are those by the famous calligraphers from the Tang Dynasty (618-907). The inscriptions on these steles are historical materials. The "Stele of the Nestorian in China," and the "Stele of Monk Amoghavajra in the Tang Dynasty" and others provide important data for studying the relations between China and other countries. The Forest of Steles in Xi'an is praised as a treasure house of the Oriental culture and the most ancient treasure house of stone carved calligraphic works which provides valuable materials for study-

3

2

ing Chinese history, calligraphy and painting.

The Stele of Classic of Filial Piety on Stone Platform 《石台孝经》stands by the entrance to the Forest of Steles and is the first huge stele among those in Xi'an. It was engraved in 745 and the inscription was written by the Tang Emperor Xuanzong. The first part is the *Preface to the Classic of Filial Piety* which expresses the emperor's aspiration to administer the country with filial piety. The second part is the original text of the *Classic of Filial Piety* edited by Zeng Sheng, a disciple of Confucius. This stele is composed of four stones standing on stone platforms, so the name of the stele.

The Stele of Kaicheng Classics 《开成石经》 is displayed in the first exhibition room. The 13 classics are engraved on both sides of 114 stones, including *The Book of Changes, Book of Documents, The Book of Songs, Ritual of Zhou, The Book of Rites, Classic of Filial Piety, The Analects of Confucius, Literary Expositor* and *Mencius*. The last one was added in the Qing Dynasty.

These classics involve more than 600,000 words and constitute a huge treasure house of stone-carved books. They were carved in 837 or the second year of the Kaicheng reign of the Tang Dynasty, so the stele has its name. These classics are the must-read books of Confucianism. Owing to underdeveloped printing in the Tang Dynasty and to avoid mistakes in copying them by disciples, these classics were engraved on stones and were erected in the Directorate of Education in Chang'an (today's Xi'an) as standard texts. Objectively, they have played an important role in preservation and popularization of Chinese ancient culture.

The Stele of the Daqin Nestorian in China《大秦景致流行中国碑》is displayed in the second exhibition room. This stone tablet is 353 centimeters high and 103 centimeters wide and was carved in 781 or the second year of the Jianzhong reign of Emperor Dezong of the Tang Dynasty. Daqin, or Eastern Roman, then embraced Syria, Arabic Peninsular, Iraq and other countries. Nestorian was a section of Christianity and was founded by Nestorian, a Syrian. Originally, he was an Eastern Roman clergyman. He had different views about Lady Mary with Roman Church and established Nestorian in Persia. Nestorian spread to Chang'an in 635 or the ninth year of the Zhengguan reign of Emperor Taizong of the Tang Dynasty. This stele records down in Chinese and Syrian languages how the Nestorian was introduced to China through Central Asia. On the top of the stele there is a cross in memory of the death of Jesus. On the top of the stele there carved the title of the stele. The inscription explains when the envoy of the Nestorian arrived at Chang'an, Tang Emperor Taizong sent his minister to meet the envoy on the outskirts of Chang'an and allowed the building of the Daqin Temple in Chang'an. Also Tang Emperor Taizong ordered the construction of Nestorian temples in all prefectures. Tang Emperors Xuanzong and Shuzong treated the Nestorian. The Daqin Church sent envoys on several occasions to Chang'an to carry out activities or contribute presents. It also introduces the aim and ceremony of the Nestorian and its activities in the 150 ruling years of the Tang Dynasty. These historical events could not be found in Chinese and foreign historical books and are of great value.

Calligraphic Steles 书体石碑 are displayed in the third exhibition room. Chinese calligraphy boasts a long history in five basic script forms, namely seal script, clerical script, regular script, running script and cursive

script. Forest of Steles in Xi'an houses collections of high value for exploring Chinese calligraphy including the famous *Thousand-Word Text*, a text used in ancient times for elementary education, in running script by Tang Huaisu, *Cutting Thousand-Word Text* by Zhang Xu. Zhang's wildly running style, which is bold and developed from Tang Huaisu's, has brought great influence to the late generations. Zhang always shouted and walked wildly after he was drunken and then created calligraphic works in an unstrained style. After he dispelled the effects of alcohol, even he himself could not recognize the words he wrote.

Stone Sculpture Gallery 西安石刻艺术室 was built in 1963 and collected the stone carvings scattered in all parts of the province for preservation and study. All stone carvings fall into two categories: mausoleum stone sculpture and religious stone sculpture. This room displays 90 huge stone sculptures including two-face animal sculpture from the Eastern Han Dynasty, and squat lion, rhino, warrior, Buddha and especially four stone horses from the Tang Dynasty are of great values of culture, history and art. Other two stone horses were shipped to the United States in 1914 and collected by the Oriental Art Room of the Museum of Pennsylvania University in Philadelphia.

---

① Forest of Steles in Xi'an
② *The Stele of Classic of Filial Piety on Stone Platform*
③ *The Stele of the Daqin Nestorian In China*
④ Calligraphic stetes
⑤ *The Stele of Kaicheng Classics*
⑥ Stone Sulpture Gallery

责任编辑：谭　燕
责任印制：冯冬青
装帧设计：吴　涛
摄　　影：卞志武　谭　明　张肇基　杨　茵　陆　岩　陈克寅　王津贵
　　　　　周沁军　杨　洋　王文波　姜景余　王　燕　董　立　杜飞豹
　　　　　（部分图片由中国图片网、北京全景视觉网络科技有限公司和中
　　　　　国新闻网提供，在此表示感谢！）

图书在版编目(CIP)数据

中国奇观：英文 ／ 杜飞豹，杜明伦著．—北京：中国旅游出版社，
2007.8
　　ISBN 978-7-5032-3210-7

Ⅰ．中…Ⅱ．①杜…②杜… Ⅲ．①自然地理—概况—中国—英文
②人文地理—概况—中国—英文 Ⅳ．K92

中国版本图书馆 CIP 数据核字(2007) 第 099930 号

审图号：GS(2007)876 号

书　　名：中国奇观(英文)

作　　者：杜飞豹　　杜明伦
译　　者：匡佩华　任玲娟　于　曼
出版发行：中国旅游出版社
　　　　　（北京建国门内大街甲9号　邮政编码：100005）
　　　　　http://www.cttp.net.com　E-mail:cttp@cnta.gov.cn
　　　　　发行部电话：010-85166507　85166517
经　　销：全国各地新华书店
印　　刷：精美彩色印刷有限公司
版　　次：2007年8月第1版　2007年8月第1次印刷
开　　本：720毫米×970毫米　1/16
印　　张：19.25
印　　数：1-5000 册
字　　数：250千
定　　价：98.00元
ＩＳＢＮ　978-7-5032-3210-7

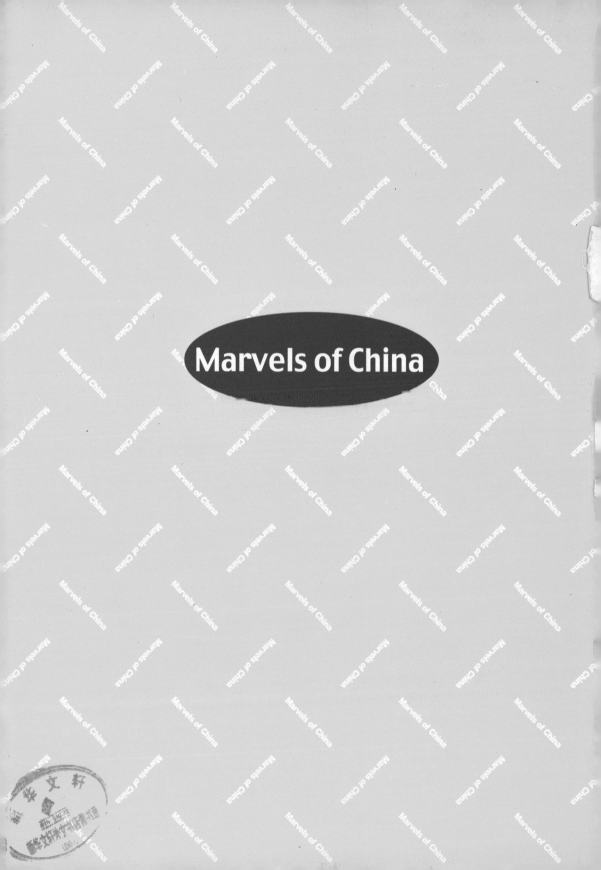